Schöningh

EinFach Englisch

Utopia and Dystopia

Exploring Alternative Worlds

Edited by
Hauke Hoffmann and Andrea Steen

Series Editor:
Hans Kröger

Sprachliche Betreuung: Simone Duxbury-Ziemer

www.schoeningh-schulbuch.de
Schöningh Verlag, Jühenplatz 1–3, 33098 Paderborn

Druck 5 4 3 2 / Jahr 2015 14 13 12 11
Die letzte Zahl bezeichnet das Jahr dieses Druckes.

Umschlaggestaltung: Jennifer Kirchhof
Druck und Bindung: westermann druck GmbH, Braunschweig

ISBN 978-3-14-041202-5

Contents

Getting started 5

I. The beginnings

- Beat swords into plowshares: Book of Isaiah (ca. 700 B.C.) **8**
- Fruits piled one above another and virgin-pure Companions: The Qur'an (early 7th century A.D.) **9**
- The greatest happiness of the whole: Plato, The Republic (360 B.C.) **11**
- Sacred marriages: Plato, The Republic (360 B.C.) **14**

II. The classics: Utopia – life as it should be

- Till death do us part: Thomas More, Utopia (1516) **16**
- The coupling of males and females: Tommaso Campanella, The City of the Sun (1602) **18**
- Perfected education: Jonathan Swift, Gulliver's Travels (1726) **20**

III. The modern classics: Dystopia – nightmare worlds

- The sunset of mankind: H.G. Wells, The Time Machine (1895) **23**
- The secret of happiness and virtue: Aldous Huxley, Brave New World (1932) **28**
- Freedom is slavery: George Orwell, 1984 (1948) **37**

IV. The present

- After the catastrophe: Margaret Atwood, The Handmaid's Tale (1985) **41**
- It is the world that has been pulled over your eyes to blind you from the truth: Larry and Andy Wachowski, The Matrix (1996) **52**
- Bonfire: Margaret Atwood, Oryx and Crake (2003) **63**

- Paradice project: Margaret Atwood, Oryx and Crake (2003) **66**
- The dimples of DelGlacey: M.T. Anderson, Feed (2004) **70**
- I love my wife: Robert Sheckley, The Perfect Woman (1953) **75**

V. Utopia or dystopia in poetry and song

- Guess it's time for the Judgement Day: Zager and Evans, In the Year 2525 (1969) **79**
- Hey Mr. Dinosaur: The Police, Walking in Your Footsteps (1983) **81**
- It starts with an earthquake: REM, It's the End of the World (As We Know It) (1987) **83**
- This is my nirvana: Alanis Morissette, Utopia (2002) **85**
- I don't want my daddy leaving home tonight: Faithless, Mass Destruction (2004) **86**
- Thou art past the tyrant's stroke: William Shakespeare, Fear No More the Heat o' the Sun (ca. 1609) **88**

Definitions 89

Acknowledgements 91

Getting started

Hieronymus Bosch (ca. 1450–1516),
Triptych of *The Last Judgement*[1] (central panel),
Akademie der Bildenden Künste, Vienna

1. According to Bosch, what will happen on Judgement Day?
2. What might the damned in the painting have done to deserve their fate?
3. You probably have an idea of the alternative, too. What will be the destiny of the blessed? Give details, please.
4. As you can see in this painting, Bosch loved to go into details. For him and his contemporaries "hell" was considered to be the most horrible place imaginable. It was a place which people feared all their lives, whereas "heaven" was an ideal everybody tried to reach. What would be "heaven" or "hell" for you? You can either draw a picture or write a short text.

[1] According to the earliest Christian theology, a future time will come when there will be a day of judgement for all humanity. On this day, God will raise all human beings from the dead and judge them, either to eternal damnation in hell or to an eternal life in heaven.

I. The beginnings

plowshare cutting blade of a plow

Beat swords into plowshares
Book of Isaiah

Very little is known about Isaiah (*765), the greatest religious leader and prophet of his time. He was a priest for at least 58 years, from before 739 to after 686 B.C.

Like all prophets, he regarded himself as a spokesman for God, who received His messages through visions, dreams, and states of ecstasy.

His prophecies contain warnings, threats and pronouncements of punishment of the chosen people for not obeying the Lord's will. Yet they also include promises of liberation and the description of life after God's apocalyptic cleansing of the earth.

apocalyptic referring to the end of the world
exalted elevated, raised up
ye Old English for 'you' (plural)

Jacob third patriarch in the Old Testament, son of Isaac, father of the twelve tribes of Israel
Zion hill in Jerusalem and site of Solomon's temple

2:2 And it shall come to pass in the last days, that the mountain of the LORD'S house shall be established in the top of the mountains, and shall be exalted above the hills; and all nations shall flow unto it.

2:3 And many people shall go and say, Come ye and let us go up to the mountain of the Lord, to the house of the God of Jacob; and he will teach us of his ways, and we will walk in his paths: for out of Zion shall go forth the law, and the word of the LORD from Jerusalem.

to rebuke to reproach, scold

pruning hook tool for trimming trees and high bushes

2:4 And he shall judge among the nations, and shall rebuke many people: and they shall beat their swords into plowshares, and their spears into pruning hooks: nation shall not lift up sword against nation, neither shall they learn war any more.

★**to dwell** to live, reside
kid young goat

What will the relationship between man and animal be like?

fatling calf fattened for slaughter
asp venomous snake
weaned child child who is not breastfed any longer
cockatrice type of poisonous snake

11:6 The wolf also shall dwell with the lamb, and the leopard shall lie down with the kid; and the calf and the young lion and the fatling together; and a little child shall lead them.

11:7 And the cow and the bear shall feed; their young ones shall lie down together; and the lion shall eat straw like the ox.

11:8 And the sucking child shall play on the hole of the asp, and the weaned child shall put his hand on the cockatrice' den.

35:4 Say to them that are of a fearful heart, Be strong, fear not: behold, your God will come with vengeance, even with a recompence; he will come and save you.
35:5 Then the eyes of the blind shall be opened, and the ears of the deaf shall be unstopped.
35:6 Then shall the lame man leap as an hart, and the tongue of the dumb sing; for in the wilderness shall waters break out, and streams in the desert.
35:7 And the parched ground shall become a pool, and the thirsty land springs of water; in the habitation of jackals, where each lay, shall be grass with reeds and rushes. [...]
35:9 No lion shall be there, nor any ravenous beast shall go up thereon, it shall not be found there; but the redeemed shall walk there.

vengeance punishment (here: of the Israelites' numerous enemies)
recompence *Vergeltung*

In what respect will the living conditions of the Israelites be different after Judgement Day?

hart *Hirsch*

parched dry

jackals *Schakale*

reeds *Schilf*
rushes a kind of green grass
ravenous very hungry
the redeemed people delivered from sin or evil

Fruits piled one above another and virgin-pure Companions
The Qur'an

The prophet of the Islam, Muhammad, was born in Makkah, present-day Saudi Arabia, in 569 A.D. He was forty years old when, one night towards the end of the month of Ramadan, he heard the voice of an angel, who announced that God had chosen him as his messenger. Step by step, the entire Qur'an was revealed to him and he began preaching. Muhammad died in 632 A.D., the year 10 of the Islamic calendar.

Islam "Islam" means total submission to the will of Allāh
Ramadan the holy month of fasting, the ninth month of the Muslim year

[...] But give glad tidings to those who believe and work righteousness, that their portion is Gardens, beneath which rivers flow. Every time they are fed with fruits therefrom, they say: "Why, this is what we were fed with before," for they are given things in similitude; and they have therein companions pure and holy; and they abide therein for ever. (Sura 2, 25)

Here is a Parable of the Garden which the righteous are promised: in it are rivers of water incorruptible, rivers of milk of which the taste never changes; rivers of wine, a joy to those who drink; and rivers of honey pure and clean. In it there are for them all kinds of fruits; and Grace from their Lord. [...] (Sura 47, 15)

What will life after death be like for the righteous?

tidings news, messages
righteousness honesty, justness, morality
portion here: something given to them as a reward
therefrom outdated: from there
similitude similarity, likeness
to abide to live, dwell

Sura chapter of the Qur'an

Parable here: short description
incorruptible here: clean, pure and unpollutable

Gracious *gnädig*

The "Event inevitable" = Judgement Day (also called Doomsday): From the earliest times on, Jewish, Christian and Islamic theology have believed that in the future there will be a day of judgement for all humanity: both the living and the deceased.

There will … coming (ll. 3/4) no one shall doubt that it will happen
Many will bring it low many will fall down, i.e. go to hell
to exalt *verherrlichen*
scattered dispersed, spread
abroad here: widely, broadly
ye Old English for 'you' (plural)
sorted grouped
Foremost first in place
Hereafter life after death
Bliss happiness, joy
from those of old people who lived in former times

What will be offered to the righteous in Paradise?

Thrones (pl) other translators use "couches" or "beds"
encrusted covered, coated
reclining lying and resting
perpetual permanent, eternal
goblet large cup
beaker mug, cup
intoxication drunkenness
fowl chicken
lustrous shiny, splendid
pearls well-guarded eyes like valuable pearls
frivolity foolishness, silliness
taint trace of something bad
ill here: sin

Lote-tree large, thorny tree with cherry-like fruit
Talh tree a kind of acacia tree

★ **abundance** plentifullness, richness
season here: harvest time
supply here: consumption, eating

In the name of Allah, Most Gracious, Most Merciful.
When the Event inevitable cometh to pass,
There will no soul entertain falsehood concerning its coming.
Many will bring it low; many will it exalt;
When the earth shall be shaken to its depths,
And the mountains shall be crumbled to atoms,
Becoming dust scattered abroad.
And ye shall be sorted out into three classes;
Then there will be the Companions of the Right Hand –
what will be the Companions of the Right Hand?
And the Companions of the Left Hand –
what will be the Companions of the Left Hand?
And those Foremost in Faith will be Foremost in the Hereafter
These will be those Nearest to Allah:
In Gardens of Bliss:
A number of people from those of old
And a few from those of later times.
They will be on Thrones encrusted with gold and precious stones,
Reclining on them, facing each other.
Round about them will serve youths of perpetual freshness,
With goblets, shining beakers and cups filled out of clear-flowing fountains:
No after-ache will they receive therefrom, nor will they suffer from intoxication:
And with fruits, any that they may select:
And the flesh of fowls, any that they may desire;
And there will be Companions with beautiful, big, and lustrous eyes –
Like unto Pearls well-guarded.
A Reward for the Deeds of their past life.
Not frivolity will they hear therein nor any taint of ill
Only the saying, 'Peace, Peace!'
The Companions of the Right Hand – what will be the Companions of the Right Hand?
They will be among Lote-trees without thorns,
Among Talh trees with flowers of fruits piled one above another –
In shade long-extended,
By water flowing constantly,
And fruit in abundance.
Whose season is not limited, nor supply forbidden
And Thrones of Dignity, raised high.

We have created their Companions of special creation.
And made them virgin-pure and undefiled
Beloved by nature, equal in age –
For the Companions of the Right Hand.
A goodly number from those of old,
And a goodly number from those of later times.
The Companions of the Left Hand – what will be the
Companions of the Left Hand?
They will be in the midst of a fierce Blast of Fire and in
Boiling Water,
And in the shades of Black Smoke:
Nothing will be there to refresh, not to please [...]
(Sura 56, 1–44)

What kind of "Companions" will they have?

Companions here: companions of the opposite sex
undefiled untouched, pure

What will life be like for sinners?

Blast explosion or strong wind

The greatest happiness of the whole
Plato: The Republic

The Greek philosopher Plato (ca. 428–348 B.C.) founded the Academy, one of the great philosophical schools of antiquity. His thoughts had enormous impact on the development of Western philosophy. His acquaintance with Socrates, in particular his methods and arguments, altered the course of Plato's life and Socrates became one of his closest associates.
In *The Republic*, written 360 B.C, Plato – among other topics – deals with elements of an ideal state.
In Book III, Plato explains that the ideal state, the "kallipolis", is governed by "guardians", who are aided by "auxiliaries". The guardians have to go through various tests which are intended to determine which of them stays steadfast in his loyalty to the city. The guardians all live together in housing provided for them by the city. They receive no salary and can hold no possessions of their own because if they were permitted to acquire private property, they would sooner or later abuse their power and begin to rule for their own profit, rather than for the good of the entire city.
At the beginning of book IV, Adeimantus and Plato interrupt Socrates to point out that being a ruler sounds unpleasant. Since the ruler has no private wealth, he can never own land, build a house, take a trip, keep a mistress, entertain guests or take part in other activities that people think make them happy. Socrates contradicts him:

antiquity the ancient past, esp. the times of the Greeks and the Romans

The Socratic method (also called the maieutic method) is one of the oldest and most powerful teaching tactics for fostering critical thinking. Its most important peculiarity is that the philosopher teaches by asking, not by telling. It is a negative method of hypotheses elimination, in that better hypotheses are found by steadily identifying and eliminating those which lead to contradictions.

Adeimantus Plato's brother, one of the dilettante philosophers that enable Socrates to make use of his method and present his arguments

According to Plato, ➲ what is the ultimate aim of "kallipolis"?

★ **to inquire** to investigate, look into
to fashion to shape, form

[...] in establishing our city, we aren't aiming to make any one group outstandingly happy but to make the whole city so, as far as possible. We thought that we'd find justice most easily in such a city and injustice, by contrast, in the one that is governed worst, and that, by observing both cities, we'd be able to judge the question we've been inquiring into for so long. We take ourselves, then, to be fashioning the happy city, not picking out a few happy people and putting them in it, but making the whole city happy. [...]

to object to protest

to clothe to dress
to festoon to decorate
jewelry normal spelling: jewellery

Why is too much happiness ➲ of the "guardians" particularly harmful?

to give rise to to cause to exist
cobbler *Schuster*
★ **hence** therefore

Suppose, then, that someone came up to us while we were painting a statue and objected that, because we had painted the eyes (which are the most beautiful part) black rather than purple, we had not applied the most beautiful colours to the most beautiful parts of the statue. We'd think it reasonable to offer the following defense: "You mustn't expect us to paint the eyes so beautifully that they no longer appear to be eyes at all, and the same with the other parts. Rather must you look to see whether by dealing with each part appropriately, we are making the whole statue beautiful." Similarly, you mustn't force us to give our guardians the kind of happiness that would make them something other than guardians. We know how to clothe the farmers in purple robes, festoon them with gold jewelry, and tell them to work the land whenever they please. We know how to settle our potters on couches by the fire, feasting and passing the wine around, with their wheel beside them for whenever they want to make pots. And we can make all the others happy in the same way, so that the whole city is happy. Don't urge us to do this, however, for if we do, a farmer wouldn't be a farmer, not a potter a potter, and none of the others would keep to the patterns of work that give rise to a city. Now if cobblers become inferior and corrupt and claim to be what they are not, that won't do much harm to the city. Hence, as far as they and the others like them are concerned, our argument carries less weight. But if the guardians of our laws and city are merely believed to be guardians but are not, you surely see that they'll destroy the city utterly, just as they alone have the opportunity to govern it well and make it happy.

banqueter guest at a feast

If we are making true guardians, then, who are least likely to do evil to the city, and if the one who brought the charge is talking about farmers and banqueters who are happy as they would be at a festival rather than in a city, then he isn't talking about a city at all, but about something else. With this in mind, we should consider whether in setting up our guardians we are aiming to give them the greatest happiness, or whether – since our aim is to see that the city as a whole has the greatest happiness – we must compel and persuade the auxiliaries and guardians to follow our other policy and be the best possible craftsmen at their own work, and the same with all the others.

In this way, with the whole city developing and being governed well, we must leave it to nature to provide each group with its share of happiness.

I think you put that very well, he said.

Will you also think that I'm putting things well when I make the next point, which is closely akin to this one?

Which one exactly?

Consider whether or not the following things corrupt the other workers, so that they become bad.

What things?

Wealth and poverty.

How do they corrupt the other workers?

Like this. Do you think that a potter who has become wealthy will still be willing to pay attention to his craft?

Not at all.

Won't he be more idle than he was?

Much more.

Then won't he be a worse potter?

Far worse.

And surely if poverty prevents him from having tools or any of the other things he needs for his craft, he'll produce poorer work and will teach his sons, or anyone else he teaches, to be worse craftsmen.

Of course.

So poverty and wealth make a craftsman and his products worse.

Apparently.

It seems, then, that we've found other things that our guardians must guard against in every way, to prevent them from slipping into the city unnoticed.

What are they?

Both wealth and poverty. The former makes for luxury, idleness, and revolution; the latter for slavishness, bad work, and revolution as well. […]

★**to compel** to force, influence

★**craftsman** skilled worker, expert

➔ What is the ideal amount of personal happiness?

he i.e. Adeimantus

I i.e. Sokrates

akin related, connected, similar

★**idle** lazy, worthless

★**apparently** evidently, obviously

➔ Why should wealth and poverty be avoided in "kallipolis"?

to make for to cause

slavishness working like a slave

Sacred marriages
Plato: The Republic

In Book V, Socrates makes the revolutionary proposal that men and women with the same natural abilities should receive the same education and training and do the same kind of work. Hence, there will be female guardians and rulers in kallipolis as well as male ones. Their education will even take place in the same rooms.

physical training In ancient Greece, physical exercise was always performed naked.

innate inborn, natural

Glaucon another brother of Plato's, here Socrates' interlocutor

What, according to Plato, is a sacred marriage?

promiscuity having sex with many different partners
impious ungodly, sinful
beneficial of advantage
flock large group of animals or people
mating animal copulation
to breed *züchten*

prime state of perfection or highest possible quality

to hold true to be true of

[...] And since they have common dwellings and meals, rather than private ones, and live together and mix together both in physical training and in the rest of their upbringing, they will, I suppose, be driven by innate necessity to have sex with one another. Or don't you think we're talking about necessities here?
[...] But the next point, Glaucon, is that promiscuity is impious in a city of happy people, and the rulers won't allow it.
No, for it isn't right.
Then it's clear that our next task must be to make marriage as sacred as possible. And the sacred marriages will be those that are most beneficial?
Absolutely.
How, then, will they be most beneficial? Tell me this, Glaucon: I see that you have hunting dogs and quite a flock of noble fighting birds at home. Have you noticed anything about their mating and breeding?
Like what?
In the first place, although they're all noble, aren't there some that are the best and prove themselves to be so?
There are.
Do you breed them all alike, or do you try to breed from the best as much as possible?
I try to breed from the best.
And do you breed from the youngest or the oldest or from those in their prime?
From those in their prime.
And do you think that if they weren't bred in this way, your stock of birds and dogs would get much worse?
I do.
What about horses and other animals? Are things any different with them?
It would be strange if they were.
Dear me! If this also holds true of human beings, our need for excellent rulers is indeed extreme. [...] It follows from our

previous agreement, first, that the best men must have sex with the best women as frequently as possible, while the opposite is true for the most inferior men and women, and, second, that if our herd is to be of the highest possible quality, the former's offspring must be reared but not the latter's. And this must all be brought about without being noticed by anyone except the rulers, so that our herd of guardians remains as free from dissension as possible.

That's absolutely right.

Therefore certain festivals and sacrifices will be established by law at which we'll bring the brides and grooms together, and we'll direct our poets to compose appropriate hymns for the marriages that take place. We'll leave the number of marriages for the rulers to decide, but their aim will be to keep the number of males as stable as they can, taking into account war, disease, and similar factors, so that his city will, as far as possible, become neither too big nor too small.

That's right.

Then there'll have to be some sophisticated lotteries introduced, so that for each marriage the inferior people we mentioned will blame luck rather than the rulers when they aren't chosen.

There will.

And among other prizes and rewards the young men who are good in war or other things must be given permission to have sex with the women more often, since this will also be a good pretext for having them father as many of the children as possible.

That's right.

And then, as the children are born, they'll be taken over by the officials appointed for the purpose, who may be either men or women or both, since our offices are open to both sexes.

Yes.

I think they'll take the children of good parents to the nurses in charge of the rearing pen situated in a separate part of the city, but the children of inferior parents, or any child of the others that is born defective, they'll hide in a secret and unknown place that is appropriate. [...]

Why should some men and women have sex often, others rarely?

former's i.e. the best men's and women's
★**offspring** children
to rear to raise, to bring up
dissension conflict, disagreement

What is the ultimate aim of marriages?

★**sophisticated** complex, complicated

pretext excuse, alibi
to father *erzeugen*

rearing pen here: institutions to bring up these children
defective here: handicapped, disabled, disfigured

What is supposed to happen to the "offspring" of each group? Why?

they'll hide ... appropriate Without doubt, Plato is recommending infanticide by abandonment for these babies, a practice which was common in ancient Greece as a method of birth control.

II. The classics: Utopia – life as it should be

Thomas More

The word "**Utopia**", a derivative of the Greek word for "non-existing place", was coined by Thomas More himself. In this way, he can rightfully be considered to be the father of utopian literature.

Till death do us part

Thomas More: Utopia

Thomas More, 1478–1535, English humanist and statesman, exemplifies the political and spiritual uproar of the Reformation. He was beheaded for opposing the religious policies of Henry VIII.

In his famous book "De optimo rei publicae statu deque nova insula Utopia", written in Latin and first published in 1516 in France, he gives a description of the best of all possible states, whose people enjoy perfection in government, law, social life and the freest toleration of religion on an imaginary island called "Utopia".

Part VII: "Of their slaves, and of their marriages"

warrant licence
reproach accusation, blame

Why are the marriage rules so strict?

vagrant changeable, random
to venture to dare, risk

grave serious, solemn
matron here: old woman

How are spouses chosen? Why does the narrator consider this method, on the one hand, ridiculous, yet on the other reasonable and even wise?

"Their women are not married before eighteen nor their men before two-and-twenty, and if any of them run into forbidden embraces before marriage they are severely punished, and the privilege of marriage is denied them unless they can obtain a special warrant from the Prince. Such disorders cast a great reproach upon the master and mistress of the family in which they happen, for it is supposed that they have failed in their duty. The reason of punishing this so severely is, because they think that if they were not strictly restrained from all vagrant appetites, very few would engage in a state in which they venture the quiet of their whole lives, by being confined to one person, and are obliged to endure all the inconveniences with which it is accompanied. In choosing their wives they use a method that would appear to us very absurd and ridiculous, but it is constantly observed among them, and is accounted perfectly consistent with wisdom. Before marriage some grave matron presents the bride, naked, whether she is a virgin or a widow, to the bridegroom, and after that some grave man presents the bridegroom, naked, to the bride. We, indeed, both laughed at this, and condemned it as very indecent. But they, on the other hand, wondered at the folly of the men of all other nations, who, if they are but to buy a horse of a small value, are so cautious that they will see every part of him, and take off both his saddle and all his other tackle, that there may be no secret ulcer hid under any of them, and that yet in the choice of a wife, on which depends the happiness or unhappiness of the rest of his life, a man should venture upon trust, and only see about a handsbreadth of the face, all the rest of the body being covered, under which may lie hid what may be contagious as well as loathsome. All men are not so wise as to choose a woman only for her good qualities, and even wise men consider the body as that which adds not a little to the mind, and it is certain there may be some such deformity covered with clothes as may totally alienate a man from his wife, when it is too late to part with her; if such a thing is discovered after marriage a man has no remedy but patience; they, therefore, think it is reasonable that there should be good provision made against such mischievous frauds.

"There was so much the more reason for them to make a regulation in this matter, because they are the only people of those parts that neither allow of polygamy nor of divorces, except in the case of adultery or insufferable perverseness, for in these cases the Senate dissolves the marriage and grants the injured person leave to marry again; but the guilty are made infamous and are never allowed the privilege of a second marriage. None are suffered to put away their wives against their wills, from any great calamity that may have fallen on their persons, for they look on it as the height of cruelty and treachery to abandon either of the married persons when they need most the tender care of their consort, and that chiefly in the case of old age, which, as it carries many diseases along with it, so it is a disease of itself. But it frequently falls out that when a married couple do not well agree, they, by mutual consent, separate, and find out other persons with whom they hope they may live more happily; yet this is not done without obtaining leave of the Senate, which never admits of a divorce but upon a strict inquiry made, both by the senators and their wives, into the grounds upon which it is desired, and even when they are satisfied concerning the reasons of it they go on but slowly, for they imagine that too great easiness in granting leave for new marriages would very much shake the kindness of married people. They punish severely those that defile the marriage bed; ...

tackle *Zaumzeug*

ulcer *Geschwür*

* **contagious** infectious, transmissible

loathsome repulsive, disgusting

* **to alienate** to separate, isolate

mischievous destructive, harmful

fraud trickery, cheating

those parts i.e. this (hypothetical) part of the world

Under which circumstances and regulations are divorces possible?

* **polygamy** having more than one married partner

* **adultery** infidelity

When would divorces never be allowed by the authorities?

consort married partner, spouse

mutual consent agreement from both sides

to obtain leave to get permission

to defile to soil, pollute, here: commit adultery

The coupling of males and females
Tommaso Campanella: The City of the Sun

Tommaso Campanella

Tommaso Campanella (1568–1639), Italian philosopher, political theorist, scientist, astrologer and poet had been influenced by More's travel account when he wrote his book *La Città del Sole (The City of the Sun)*. Hence there are striking similarities between the two utopias.
Campanella composed his "Dialogo Poetico" (poetical dialogue) while imprisoned in Naples for his part in a rebellion against the Spanish and Catholic authorities who ruled his native Calabria.
Like *Utopia*, it is also mainly narrated by a sailor who has seen ideal conditions existing on a far away island.
Campanella's emphasis on education for everyone and the importance of studying the sciences are two very notable Renaissance characteristics of this book.

A poetical dialogue between a Grandmaster of the Knights Hospitalers and a Genoese Sea-Captain, his guest.

What is the ultimate purpose of having sex in the City of the Sun?

Love one of the rulers of the City of the Sun

GENOESE: Love has charge of breeding and sees to the coupling of males and females who will produce healthy offspring. They laugh at us because we are careful about the breeding of dogs and horses while we pay no attention to our own breeding, [...] No female ever submits to a male until she is nineteen years of age, nor does any male seek to have children until he is twenty-one or, if he is pale and delicate, even older. Before that age some of them are permitted to have intercourse with barren or pregnant women so as to avoid illicit usages. [...]
Since both males and females, in the manner of the ancient Greeks, are completely naked when they engage in their wrestling exercises, their teachers may readily distinguish those who are able to have intercourse from those who are not and can determine whose sexual organs may best be matched with whose. Consequently, every third night, after they have all bathed, the young people are paired off for intercourse. Tall, handsome girls are not matched with any but tall, brave men, while fat girls are matched with thin men and thin girls with fat ones, so as to avoid extremes in their offspring. On the appointed evening, the boys and girls prepare their beds and go to bed where the matron and senior direct them. Nor may

delicate fragile, here: weak

to have intercourse here: to have sex
barren infertile, unproductive
illicit illegal, unlawful
usage practice, custom

According to what criteria are young people „matched"?

The **matron** and the **senior** are the young people's supervisors.

they have intercourse until they have completely digested their food and have said their prayers. [...]

When a woman has conceived, she avoids all exercise for fifteen days. Then she begins to take only light exercise so as to strengthen the unborn infant and to open to it the channels of nourishment. Once it is born, the mother suckles it and cares for it herself in a public nursery for a period of two years or longer, according to the judgment of the Physical Scientist. After being weaned, the child is put into the care of teachers – male or female, according to the child's sex. Here, in the company of other children, he studies the alphabet and the paintings on the wall and also learns to walk, run, and wrestle. Children wear clothes of various pleasant colors. At the age of seven they are directed to the natural sciences and then to the other sciences as the officials determine. After this, they take up the mechanical arts. Those who demonstrate little ability are sent out into the country. When they improve, they are brought back to the city. But in general, since those of the same age are all born under the same constellation, they tend to be alike in ability, habits, and appearance. This accounts for the concord and stability in the state and encourages the citizens to love and help each other. [...]

HOSPITALER: Is there no jealousy among them or hurt at not being chosen for parenthood? Is there no coveting?

GENOESE: Sir, there is none, for no necessity to their pleasure is lacking, and the rules governing procreation are religiously observed for public, not for private ends. Moreover, there is no need to obey official orders. Plato said that it would be necessary to trick undeserving men who felt they had a right to beautiful women by managing the drawing of lots in such a way that only deserving would win such women. But in the City of the Sun there is no need to cheat so as to match ugly men with ugly women, for there are no ugly ones among them. By exercising, the women develop lively complexions and large, strong limbs; and among these people tallness, liveliness, and strength are the attributes of beauty. It is a capital offence for women to use cosmetics, however, or to wear high heels and gowns with trains to cover the heels. But actually there is no need to forbid these things, for where would they get them? They claim that such abuses exist among us because of the idleness of our women, which makes them pale, fragile, and short and creates a need for artificial coloring, high heels, and beauty care. Thus our women ruin their constitutions and that of

to conceive to become pregnant

★ **infant** child

★ **nourishment** food, nutrition

to suckle to give milk, breast-feed

nursery home for babies and their mothers

to be weaned to be gradually stopped from breast-feeding

constellation here: the grouping of the stars at the moment of birth. Campanella, as an astrologer, was convinced of the influence of the constellation of the stars on the lives of people.

coveting desire, sexual jealousy

procreation *Fortpflanzung*

ends means, reasons

Plato ... women compare "Sacred marriages", pp. 14f.

complexion color and appearance of the skin

liveliness being energetic and full of life

gown here: dress

train here: *Schleppe*

➜ What are women not allowed to do? Why?

➜ Why – according to the Genoese captain – do women outside the City of the Sun apply make-up and wear high-heeled shoes? Which possible consequences of such habits are mentioned?

to become enamored of to fall in love with

Which role does love play in this society?

to jest to joke
emblem symbol
to deem to regard, consider
★**sterile** infertile, unable to bear offspring
concupiscent lustful, sexually motivated
ardour desire, passion

their children as well. If a man becomes enamored of a woman, he may speak and jest with her, send her verses, and make emblems out of flowers and branches for her. But if his having intercourse with her is deemed undesirable by reason of the offspring that might result, it will by no means be permitted unless she is already pregnant or is sterile. As a result, only loving friendship, rather than concupiscent ardour, is recognized among them. [...]

Perfected education

Jonathan Swift: Gulliver's Travels

Jonathan Swift

Jonathan Swift (1667–1745), Irish poet, political writer, and clergyman, ranks as one of the greatest satirists in world literature. From the moment of its publication in 1726, his most famous work, *Gulliver's Travels*, a satirical fantasy in the form of a travel book, has been regarded as both a delightful children's story and one of the most bitter attacks on human corruption in the English language. In the following extract from the first part of the book, called "A Voyage to Lilliput", the protagonist and first-person narrator Mr Lemuel Gulliver, an English surgeon and seaman, is shipwrecked in a storm but manages to swim to ashore. The island is inhabited by strange people not more than six inches high. The Lilliputians are soon charmed by Gulliver's friendly manner and his desire to learn their language and customs.

Chapter VI:

Notions/Duties etc.
Swift's capitalization (*Groß- und Kleinschreibung*) differs very much from Modern English and is actually rather close to German spelling.

Notion idea, opinion
Conjunction uniting, connection
to propagate to have children, reproduce
will needs have it in case it turns out to be unavoidable
Concupiscence strong sexual desire
to beget to father, sire

Their Notions relating to the Duties of Parents and Children differ extremely from ours. For since the Conjunction of Male and Female is founded upon the great Law of Nature, in order to propagate and continue the Species, the Lilliputians will needs have it, that Men and Women are joined together like other Animals, by the Motives of Concupiscence; and that their Tenderness towards their Young proceeds from the like natural Principle: for which reason they will never allow, that a Child is under any Obligation to his Father for begetting him, or his Mother for bringing him into the World; which, considering the Miseries of human Life, was neither a Benefit in it self, or intended so by his Parents, whose Thoughts in their Love-Encounters were otherwise employ'd. Upon these, and the like Reasonings, their Opinion is, that Parents are the last of all others to be trusted with the Education of their own Children: and therefore they have in every Town publick Nurseries, where all Parents, except Cottagers and Labourers, are obliged to send their Infants of both Sexes to be reared and educated when they come to the Age of twenty Moons, at which time they are supposed to have some Rudiments of Docility. These Schools are of several kinds, suited to different Qualities, and to both Sexes. They have certain Professors well skilled in preparing Children for such a condition of Life as befits the Rank of their Parents, and their own Capacities as well as Inclinations. I shall say something of the Male Nurseries, and then of the Female.

The Nurseries for Males of Noble or Eminent Birth are provided with Grave and Learned Professors, and their several Deputies. The Clothes and Food of the Children are plain and simple. They are bred up in the Principles of Honour, Justice, Courage, Modesty, Clemency, Religion, and Love of their Country; they are always employed in some Business, except in the times of Eating and Sleeping, which are very short, and two Hours for Diversions, consisting of bodily Exercises. They are dressed by Men till four Years of Age, and then are obliged to dress themselves, although their Quality be ever so great; and the Women Attendants, who are Aged proportionably to ours at fifty, perform only the most menial Offices. They are never suffered to converse with Servants, but go together in small or greater Numbers to take their diversions, and always in the presence of a Professor, or one of his Deputies; whereby they avoid those early bad Impressions of Folly and Vice to which our Children are subject. Their Parents are suffered to see them only twice a Year; the visit is to last but an hour. They are allowed to kiss the Child at Meeting and Parting; but a Professor, who always stands by on those occasions, will not suffer them to whisper, or use any fondling Expressions, or bring any Presents of Toys, Sweet-meats, and the like.

The Pension from each Family for the Education and Entertainment of a Child, upon failure of due payment, is levyed by the Emperor's Officers.

The Nurseries for Children of ordinary Gentlemen, Merchants, Traders, and Handicrafts, are managed proportionably after the same manner; only those designed for Trades, are put out Apprentices at Eleven years old, whereas those of Persons of Quality continue in their exercises till Fifteen, which answers to One and Twenty with us: but the Confinement is gradually lessened for the last three Years.

➔ Why should parents "not be trusted with the education of their own children"?

Cottager farm worker
Labourer someone who does manual work
reared raised, brought up
Rudiments (pl) here: fundamental knowledge
Docility obedience, submissiveness
to befit to be suitable for
Inclination liking, preference

Eminent famous, renowned
Grave serious, severe

Clemency mildness, leniency
Business here: activity

Diversion entertainment, distraction
to be obliged to to have to

at fifty According to Gulliver, Lilliputians, being smaller, die younger.

proportionably comparably
menial humble, inferior, low
suffered here: allowed
Folly foolishness
Vice moral corruption, immorality, bad habits

➔ What are visiting parents not allowed to do?

fondling kind, loving
Sweet-meats candy, cakes
Pension financial contribution
Entertainment here: nourishment, maintenance
to levy here: to impose, collect

Handicrafts craftsmen
are … Apprentices leave the school to become apprentices
which answers … with us which is equivalent to the age of twenty-one in our society
Confinement imprisonment, restrictions, restraints

orderly tidy, neat, well-organized

to presume to dare, venture

desolate lonely, far away, miserable

★ **to despise** to hate, loathe

What is the only difference between the education of girls and boys? ➔

Which reason is given for the differentiation? ➔

Compass curriculum
to enjoin to direct, order
★ **maxim** rule of conduct

meaner poorer, from inferior classes

Steward person overseeing the institution
Gettings income
Portion here: nourishment, food

subservience giving in, submissiveness
Burthen burden

to appropriate to set aside, allot

Husbandry management of resources

to till to plow

In the Female Nurseries, the young Girls of Quality are educated much like the Males, only they are dressed by orderly Servants of their own Sex; but always in the presence of a Professor or Deputy, till they come to dress themselves, which is at five Years old. And if it be found that these Nurses ever presume to entertain the Girls with frightful or foolish Stories, or the common Follies practiced by Chamber-Maids among us, they are publickly whipped thrice about the City, imprisoned for a Year and banished for Life to the most desolate part of the Country. Thus the young Ladies there are as much ashamed of being Cowards and Fools as the Men, and despise all personal Ornaments beyond Decency and Cleanliness: Neither did I perceive any Difference in their Education, made by their Difference of Sex, only that the Exercises of the Females were not altogether so robust; and that some Rules were given them relating to domestic Life, and a smaller Compass of Learning was enjoined them: for their maxim is, that among People of Quality a Wife should be always a reasonable and agreeable Companion, because she cannot always be young. When the Girls are twelve Years old, which among them is the marriageable Age, their Parents or Guardians take them home, with great Expressions of Gratitude to the Professors, and seldom without Tears of the young Lady and her Companions.

In the Nurseries of Females of the meaner sort, the Children are instructed in all kinds of Works proper for their Sex, and their several degrees: Those intended for Apprentices, are dismissed at nine Years old, the rest are kept to thirteen.

The meaner Families who have Children at these Nurseries, are obliged, besides their annual Pension, which is as low as possible, to return to the Steward of the Nursery a small monthly Share of their Gettings, to be a Portion for the Child; and therefore all Parents are limited in their expenses by the Law. For the Lilliputians think nothing can be more unjust, than for People, in subservience to their own Appetites, to bring Children into the World and leave the Burthen of supporting them on the Publick. As to Persons of Quality, they give Security to appropriate a certain Sum for each Child, suitable to their Condition; and these Funds are always managed with good Husbandry, and the most exact Justice.

The Cottagers and Labourers keep their Children at Home, their Business being only to till and cultivate the Earth, and therefore their Education is of little consequence to the Publick; but the Old and Diseased among them are supported by Hospitals: for Begging is a Trade unknown in this Kingdom.

III. The modern classics: Dystopia – nightmare worlds

The sunset of mankind

H. G. Wells: The Time Machine

Herbert George Wells (1866–1946) was fascinated all his life by the power of science to shape man's destiny. Science had also lifted him from the lower-middle class into which he was born. He won a scholarship to study biology under Thomas Henry Huxley, grandfather of Aldous Huxley, the author of the next text. By 1895, Wells had established himself as one of England's most popular writers, particularly of "scientific romances", the forerunner of modern science fiction. He also attained fame for his knowledge about political and social issues. A lifelong socialist, he had a great influence on the party platform of the Labour Party.

The first-person narrator of the novel has constructed a machine with which he can travel in the fourth dimension, i.e. time. His first journey takes him to the year 802,701 A.D. The world has changed considerably. In the following extract from chapter 4 of the novel, he describes his first encounter with the "Eloi", the people inhabiting the earth of that distant future.

Herbert George Wells

[...] I looked at the half-dozen little figures that were following me. Then, in a flash, I perceived that all had the same form of costume, the same soft hairless visage, and the same girlish rotundity of limb. It may seem strange, perhaps, that I had not noticed this before. But everything was so strange. Now, I saw the fact plainly enough. In costume, and in all the differences of texture and bearing that now mark off the sexes from each other, these people of the future were alike. And the children seemed to my eyes to be but the miniatures of their parents. I judged, then, that the children of that time were extremely precocious, physically at least, and I found afterwards abundant verification of my opinion.

Seeing the ease and security in which these people were living, I felt that this close resemblance of the sexes was after all what one would expect; for the strength of a man and the softness of a woman, the institution of the family, and the

visage face
rotundity roundedness

texture *Beschaffenheit*
to mark off to distinguish

precocious mature for one's age
⋆**verification** proof, confirmation

differentiation of occupations are mere militant necessities of an age of physical force; where population is balanced and abundant, much childbearing becomes an evil rather than a blessing to the State; where violence comes but rarely and offspring are secure, there is less necessity – indeed there is no necessity – for an efficient family, and the specialization of the sexes with reference to their children's needs disappears. We see some beginnings of this even in our own time, and in this future age it was complete. This, I must remind you, was my speculation at the time. Later, I was to appreciate how far it fell short of the reality.

While I was musing upon these things, my attention was attracted by a pretty little structure, like a well under a cupola. I thought in a transitory way of the oddness of wells still existing, and then resumed the thread of my speculations. There were no large buildings towards the top of the hill, and as my walking powers were evidently miraculous, I was presently left alone for the first time. With a strange sense of freedom and adventure I pushed on up to the crest.

There I found a seat of some yellow metal that I did not recognize, corroded in places with a kind of pinkish rust and half smothered in soft moss, the arm-rests cast and filed into the resemblance of griffins' heads. I sat down on it, and I surveyed the broad view of our old world under the sunset of that long day. It was as sweet and fair a view as I have ever seen. The sun had already gone below the horizon and the west was flaming gold, touched with some horizontal bars of purple and crimson. Below was the valley of the Thames, in which the river lay like a band of burnished steel. I have already spoken of the great palaces dotted about among the variegated greenery, some in ruins and some still occupied. Here and there rose a white or silvery figure in the waste garden of the earth, here and there came the sharp vertical line of some cupola or obelisk. There were no hedges, no signs of proprietary rights, no evidences of agriculture; the whole earth had become a garden.

So watching, I began to put my interpretation upon the things I had seen, and as it shaped itself to me that evening, my interpretation was something in this way. (Afterwards I found I had got only a half-truth – or only a glimpse of one facet of the truth.)

It seemed to me that I had happened upon humanity upon the wane. The ruddy sunset set me thinking of the sunset of mankind. For the first time I began to realize an odd consequence of the social effort in which we are at present en-

to muse upon to ponder on, think about
well *Brunnen*
cupola dome
transitory temporary, passing
★**to resume** to begin again, continue

crest highest point (of a mountain)

smothered thickly covered

griffin mythological creature with the wings and head of an eagle and the body of a lion

burnished polished
dotted about spread over
variegated varied
waste here: wasteful, lavish

proprietary exclusively owned, forbidden to the general public

facet aspect
upon the wane in decline
ruddy reddish

gaged. And yet, come to think, it is a logical consequence enough. Strength is the outcome of need; security sets a premium on feebleness. The work of ameliorating the conditions of life – the true civilizing process that makes life more and more secure – had gone steadily on to a climax. One triumph of a united humanity over Nature had followed another. Things that are now mere dreams had become projects deliberately put in hand and carried forward. And the harvest was what I saw!

After all, the sanitation and the agriculture of today are still in the rudimentary stage. The science of our time has attacked but a little department of the field of human disease, but even so, it spreads its operations very steadily and persistently. Our agriculture and horticulture destroy a weed just here and there and cultivate perhaps a score or so of wholesome plants, leaving the greater number to fight out a balance as they can. We improve our favourite plants and animals – and how few they are – gradually by selective breeding; now a new and better peach, now a seedless grape, now a sweeter and larger flower, now a more convenient breed of cattle. We improve them gradually, because our ideals are vague and tentative, and our knowledge is very limited; because Nature, too, is shy and slow in our clumsy hands. Some day all this will be better organized, and still better. That is the drift of the current in spite of the eddies. The whole world will be intelligent, educated, and cooperating; things will move faster and faster towards the subjugation of Nature. In the end, wisely and carefully we shall readjust the balance of animal and vegetable to suit our human needs.

This adjustment, I say, must have been done, and done well; done indeed for all Time, in the space of Time across which my machine had leaped. The air was free from gnats, the earth from weeds or fungi; everywhere were fruits and sweet and delightful flowers; brilliant butterflies flew hither and thither. The ideal of preventive medicine was attained. Diseases had been stamped out. I saw no evidence of any contagious diseases during all my stay. And I shall have to tell you later that even the processes of putrefaction and decay had been profoundly affected by these changes.

Social triumphs, too, had been effected. I saw mankind housed in splendid shelters, gloriously clothed, and as yet I had found them engaged in no toil. There were no signs of struggle, neither social nor economical struggle. The shop, the advertisement, traffic, all that commerce which consti-

➊ What does he consider to be the ultimate consequence of the social efforts of his contemporaries?

feebleness weakness
to ameliorate to improve

rudimentary elementary, not fully developed

horticulture cultivation of plants

wholesome beneficial, healthy

tentative experimental

eddy *Wirbel, Strudel*

subjugation act of bringing into submission

gnat *Mücke*

fungi *Pilze*

hither and thither from here to there

preventive medicine methods taken to stop diseases developing

putrefaction rotting

toil (hard) work

Why does he initially consider this world of the future a "social paradise"?

tutes the body of our world, was gone. It was natural on that golden evening that I should jump at the idea of a social paradise. The difficulty of increasing population had been met, I guessed, and population had ceased to increase.

The Time Traveller soon discovers that a second race inhabits this world of the distant future, loathsome, ape-like creatures, called "Morlocks". They are also descendants of the human beings of our time. The world has been divided between the fragile, childlike Eloi, who live on the surface of the earth, and the fierce, obscene Morlocks, who inhabit underground tunnels, which they only leave at night. Weena, an Eloi girl, who has become the Time Traveller's trusting and affectionate companion, is terrified of the time the Morlocks come to the surface. The following are extracts from chapter 7.

malign evil, harmful
to loathe to hate, detest

[...] there was an altogether new element in the sickening quality of the Morlocks – a something inhuman and malign. Instinctively I loathed them. Before, I had felt as a man might feel who had fallen into a pit: my concern was with the pit and how to get out of it. Now I felt like a beast in a trap, whose enemy would come upon him soon.
The enemy I dreaded may surprise you. It was the darkness of the new moon. Weena had put this into my head by some at first incomprehensible remarks about the Dark Nights. It was not now such a very difficult problem to guess what the coming Dark Nights might mean. The moon was on the wane: each night there was a longer interval of darkness. And I now understood to some slight degree at least the reason of the fear of the little Upper-world people for the dark. I wondered vaguely what foul villainy it might be that the Morlocks did under the new moon. I felt pretty sure now that my second hypothesis was all wrong. The Upper-world people might once have been the favoured aristocracy, and the Morlocks their mechanical servants: but that had long since passed away. The two species that had resulted from the evolution of man were sliding down towards, or had already arrived at, an altogether new relationship. The Eloi, like the Carolingian kings, had decayed to a mere beautiful futility. They still possessed the earth on sufferance: since the Morlocks, subterranean for innumerable generations, had come at last to find the daylit surface intolerable. And the Morlocks made their garments, I inferred, and maintained them in their habitual needs, perhaps through the survival of an old habit of service. They did it as

on the wane diminishing, becoming smaller

villainy wicked acts

Who – according to the Time Traveller – might have been the ancestors of the Eloi, who those of the Morlocks?

Carolingian kings Frankish dynasty that ruled France and Germany during the 8th – 10th centuries

futility uselessness, worthlessness
sufferance consent, permission
subterranean underground
garments (pl) clothes
to infer to conclude
habitual customary, routine

a standing horse paws with his foot, or as a man enjoys killing animals in sport: because ancient and departed necessities had impressed it on the organism. But, clearly, the old order was already in part reversed. The Nemesis of the delicate ones was creeping on apace. Ages ago, thousands of generations ago, man had thrust his brother man out of the ease and the sunshine. And now that brother was coming back changed! Already the Eloi had begun to learn one old lesson anew. They were becoming reacquainted with Fear. And suddenly there came into my head the memory of the meat I had seen in the Under-world. It seemed odd how it floated into my mind: not stirred up as it were by the current of my meditations, but coming in almost like a question from outside. I tried to recall the form of it. I had a vague sense of something familiar, but I could not tell what it was at the time.

Still, however helpless the little people in the presence of their mysterious Fear, I was differently constituted. I came out of this age of ours, this ripe prime of the human race, when Fear does not paralyse and mystery has lost its terrors. I at least would defend myself. Without further delay I determined to make myself arms and a fastness where I might sleep. With that refuge as a base, I could face this strange world with some of that confidence I had lost in realizing to what creatures night by night I lay exposed. I felt I could never sleep again until my bed was secure from them. I shuddered with horror to think how they must already have examined me.

[...] And then I thought once more of the meat that I had seen. I felt assured now of what it was, and from the bottom of my heart I pitied this last feeble rill from the great flood of humanity. Clearly, at some time in the Long-Ago of human decay the Morlocks' food had run short. Possibly they had lived on rats and such-like vermin. Even now man is far less discriminating and exclusive in his food than he was – far less than any monkey. His prejudice against human flesh is no deep-seated instinct. And so these inhuman sons of men – ! I tried to look at the thing in a scientific spirit. After all, they were less human and more remote than our cannibal ancestors of three or four thousand years ago. And the intelligence that would have made this state of things a torment had gone. Why should I trouble myself? These Eloi were mere fatted cattle, which the ant-like Morlocks preserved and preyed upon – probably saw to the breeding of. And there was Weena dancing at my side!

to paw *scharren*

Nemesis goddess of punishment and revenge in Greek mythology

on apace swiftly, quickly
to thrust to drive, push

ripe prime state of perfection
to paralyse to make immovable

arms weapons
fastness secure place

rill small brook, stream

vermin *Ungeziefer*
discriminating choosing carefully, showing taste

torment great pain, torture
to prey to hunt and kill for food

➔ What is the major nourishment of the subterranean people?

Aldous Huxley

hatchery place for hatching eggs
conditioning training process involving reward and punishment

The World State's motto, **"Community, Identity, Stability"** is an allusion to the three ideals of the French revolution: Liberté, Egalité, Fraternité

pane window glass
draped covered with cloth
lay in a horizontal position
pallid pale, colourless
***bleakly** gloomily, in a cheerless manner
tube here: hollow cylinder, pipette
luscious delicious, tasty; fertile
in recession here: one behind the other
fertilizing inseminating, making pregnant
plunged here: deeply concentrated
soliloquizing talking to oneself, reciting a monologue
callow inexperienced
abjectly in a humble manner
from the horse's mouth coming from an expert (here: the Director)
to conduct here: to lead

The secret of happiness and virtue

Aldous Huxley: Brave New World

Aldous Huxley (1894–1963) was born into a family of famous scientists and poets. He soon made a name for himself as an author of poetry, essays, short stories, travel writing and novels. The most famous and enduring of these was *Brave New World* (its title is a quotation from Shakespeare's *The Tempest*), which was published in 1932.
The following extract is the beginning of the novel.

A squat grey building of only thirty-four stories. Over the main entrance the words, Central London Hatchery and Conditioning Centre, and, in a shield, the World State's motto, Community, Identity, Stability.

The enormous room on the ground floor faced towards the north. Cold for all the summer beyond the panes, for all the tropical heat of the room itself, a harsh thin light glared through the windows, hungrily seeking some draped lay figure, some pallid shape of academic goose-flesh, but finding only the glass and nickel and bleakly shining porcelain of a laboratory. Wintriness responded to wintriness. The overalls of the workers were white, their hands gloved with a pale corpse-coloured rubber. The light was frozen, dead, a ghost. Only from the yellow barrels of the microscopes did it borrow a certain rich and living substance, lying along the polished tubes like butter, streak after luscious streak in long recession down the work tables.

'And this,' said the Director opening the door, 'is the Fertilizing Room.'

Bent over their instruments, three hundred Fertilizers were plunged, as the Director of Hatcheries and Conditioning entered the room, in the scarcely breathing silence, the absent-minded, soliloquizing hum or whistle, of absorbed concentration. A troop of newly arrived students, very young, pink and callow, followed nervously, rather abjectly, at the Director's heels. Each of them carried a note-book, in which, whenever the great man spoke, he desperately scribbled. Straight from the horse's mouth. It was a rare privilege. The D.H.C. for Central London always made a point of personally conducting his new students round the various departments. 'Just to give you a general idea,' he would explain to them. For of course some sort of general idea they must have, if they were to do their work intelligently – though as little of one, if they were to be good and happy members of society, as possible. For particulars, as every one knows, make for virtue and happiness; generalities are intellectually necessary evils. Not philosophers, but fret-sawyers and stamp collectors compose the backbone of society.

'Tomorrow,' he would add, smiling at them with a slightly menacing geniality, 'you'll be settling down to serious work. You won't have time for generalities. Meanwhile...' Meanwhile, it was a privilege. Straight from the horse's mouth into the note-book. The boys scribbled like mad.

Tall and rather thin but upright, the Director advanced into the room. He had a long chin and big, rather prominent teeth, just covered, when he was not talking, by his full, floridly curved lips. Old, young? Thirty? fifty? fifty-five? It was hard to say. And anyhow the question didn't arise; in this year of stability, a.f. 632, it didn't occur to you to ask it.

'I shall begin at the beginning,' said the D.H.C. and the more zealous students recorded his intention in their note-books: Begin at the beginning. 'These,' he waved his hand, 'are the incubators.' And opening an insulated door he showed them racks upon racks of numbered test-tubes. 'The week's supply of ova. Kept,' he explained, 'at blood heat; whereas the male gametes,' and here he opened another door, 'they have to be kept at thirty-five instead of thirty-seven. Full blood heat sterilizes.' Rams wrapped in thermogene beget no lambs. Still leaning against the incubators he gave them, while the pencils scurried illegibly across the pages, a brief description of the modern fertilizing process; spoke first, of course, of its surgical introduction – 'the operation undergone voluntarily for the good of Society, not to mention the fact that it carries a bonus amounting to six months' salary'; continued with some account of the technique for preserving the excised ovary alive and actively developing; passed on to a consideration of optimum temperature, salinity, viscosity; referred to the liquor in which the detached and ripened eggs were kept; and, leading his charges to the work tables, actually showed them how this liquor was drawn off from the test-tubes; how it was let out drop by drop on to the specially warmed slides of the microscopes; how the eggs which it contained were inspected for abnormalities, counted and transferred to a porous receptacle how (and he now took them to watch the operation) this receptacle; was immersed in a warm bouillon containing free-swimming spermatozoa – at a minimum concentration of one hundred thousand per cubic centimetre, he insisted; and how, after ten minutes, the con-

fret-sawyers in BNW, people who create ornamental works
menacing threatening, dangerous
geniality kindliness, warmth
florid bright red

a.f. after Ford, i.e. after Henry Ford (1863–1947), the founder of the Ford Motor Company, who was one of the first to apply assembly line manufacturing to the mass production of his cars

zealous excited, passionate
incubator apparatus which keeps eggs warm until they hatch
insulated isolated
***racks** (pl) shelves
ova (pl) female gametes, eggs
gametes (pl) reproductive cells

thirty-five instead of thirty-seven refers to the lower temperature in the testicles so that they can carry out their job of producing healthy sperm

ram male sheep

thermogene author-coined expression: thermo: of heat; gene: section of a chromosome which transmits hereditary characteristics

to beget to father, sire
to scurry to move quickly
illegibly unreadably
excised removed
salinity level of saltiness
viscosity thickness, stickiness
detached removed

slide *Objektträger*

receptacle container
immersed covered with liquid

What is the first difference mentioned between Alphas and Betas on the one hand, and Gammas, Deltas and Epsilons on the other?

What is the advantage of "bokanovskification"?

Bokanovsky's Process
Bokanovsky: in the book the inventor of an advanced method of cloning. The real Maurice Bokanovsky was a French politician (1879–1928).

to bud to grow buds, sprout
to proliferate to multiply
arrest here: delay, slowing down

to purr to make a low soft sound (like a satisfied cat)

susceptible vulnerable

to be dosed to be given a specified quantity of sth
to burgeon to bloom, expand

prodigious great, huge, wonderful
piddling trivial, of little value
viviparous giving birth to living young
★**scores** large numbers

largesse gift, grant, donation

tainer was lifted out of the liquor and its contents re-examined; how, if any of the eggs remained unfertilized, it was again immersed, and, if necessary, yet again; how the fertilized ova went back to the incubators; where the Alphas and Betas remained until definitely bottled; while the Gammas, Deltas and Epsilons were brought out again, after only thirty-six hours, to undergo Bokanovsky's Process.

'Bokanovsky's Process,' repeated the Director, and the students underlined the words in their little note-books.

One egg, one embryo, one adult – normality. But a bokanovskified egg will bud, will proliferate, will divide. From eight to ninety-six buds, and every bud will grow into a perfectly formed embryo, and every embryo into a full-sized adult. Making ninety-six human beings grow where only one grew before. Progress.

'Essentially,' the D.H.C. concluded, 'bokanovskification consists of a series of arrests of development. We check the normal growth and, paradoxically enough, the egg responds by budding.'

Responds by budding. The pencils were busy.

He pointed. On a very slowly moving band a rack-full of test-tubes was entering a large metal box, another rack-full was emerging. Machinery faintly purred. It took eight minutes for the tubes to go through, he told them. Eight minutes of hard X-rays being about as much as an egg can stand. A few died; of the rest, the least susceptible divided into two; most put out four buds; some eight; all were returned to the incubators, where the buds began to develop; then, after two days, were suddenly chilled, chilled and checked. Two, four, eight, the buds in their turn budded; and having budded were dosed almost to death with alcohol; consequently burgeoned again and having budded – bud out of bud out of bud were thereafter – further arrest being generally fatal – left to develop in peace. By which time the original egg was in a fair way to becoming anything from eight to ninety-six embryos – a prodigious improvement, you will agree, on nature. Identical twins – but not in piddling twos and threes as in the old viviparous days, when an egg would sometimes accidentally divide; actually by dozens, by scores at a time.

'Scores,' the Director repeated and flung out his arms, as though he were distributing largesse. 'Scores.'

But one of the students was fool enough to ask where the advantage lay.

'My good boy!' The Director wheeled sharply round on him. 'Can't you see? Can't you see?' He raised a hand; his expression was solemn. 'Bokanovsky's Process is one of the major instruments of social stability!'

Major instruments of social stability.

Standard men and women; in uniform batches. The whole of a small factory staffed with the products of a single bokanovskified egg.

'Ninety-six identical twins working ninety-six identical machines!' The voice was almost tremulous with enthusiasm. 'You really know where you are. For the first time in history.' He quoted the planetary motto. 'Community, Identity, Stability.' Grand words. 'If we could bokanovskify indefinitely the whole problem would be solved.'

Solved by standard Gammas, unvarying Deltas, uniform Epsilons. Millions of identical twins. The principle of mass production at last applied to biology.

'But, alas,' the Director shook his head, 'we can't bokanovskify indefinitely.'

Ninety-six seemed to be the limit; seventy-two a good average. From the same ovary and with gametes of the same male to manufacture as many batches of identical twins as possible – that was the best (sadly a second best) that they could do. And even that was difficult.

'For in nature it takes thirty years for two hundred eggs to reach maturity. But our business is to stabilize the population at this moment, here and now. Dribbling out twins over a quarter of a century – what would be the use of that?'

Obviously, no use at all. But Podsnap's Technique had immensely accelerated the process of ripening. They could make sure of at least a hundred and fifty mature eggs within two years. Fertilize and bokanovskify – in other words, multiply by seventy-two – and you get an average of nearly eleven thousand brothers and sisters in a hundred and fifty batches of identical twins, all within two years of the same age.

'And in exceptional cases we can make one ovary yield us over fifteen thousand adult individuals.'

Beckoning to a fair-haired, ruddy young man who happened to be passing at the moment, 'Mr. Foster,' he called. The ruddy young man approached. 'Can you tell us the record for a single ovary, Mr. Foster?'

'Sixteen thousand and twelve in this Centre,' Mr. Foster replied without hesitation. He spoke very quickly, had a vivacious blue eye, and took an evident pleasure in quoting figures. 'Sixteen thousand and twelve; in one hundred and eighty-nine batches of identicals. But of course they've done much better,' he rattled on, 'in some of the tropical Centres.

batch group of people or things

tremulous shaky, wavering

***to apply** to put to practical use

to dribble to drip, move slowly in small quantities

Mr Podsnap is a character in Dickens's *Our Mutual Friend*, who clears away all kinds of problems by saying "I don't want to know about it" or "I don't choose to discuss it". Huxley's reference to him is therefore subtly ironic.

to yield to produce

to beckon to give a sign

ruddy blushing, reddish

vivacious lively

Mombasa more common spelling: Mombassa

pituitary here: hormones produced in the pituitary (*Hirnanhangdrüse*)

to decant to pour from a bottle; here: be born

bustle lively activity

flap piece of skin

peritoneum *Bauchfell*

"Whizz" and "click" are two good examples of onomatopoeia, the formation of words which sound like the meaning they represent. Onomatopoeia is often found in comic strips.

Matriculator another author-coined term: from mater (Latin): mother

deftly skilfully

morula mass of cells in the first stage of embryonic development

labeller person who sticks on labels

heredity genetic quality of the "parents"

Social Predestination
According to Calvin and other Reformers, predestination means that God has determined the personal fate of every person in advance, especially concerning his or her salvation or damnation

★**relish** great enjoyment

Singapore has often produced over sixteen thousand five hundred; and Mombasa has actually touched the seventeen thousand mark. But then they have unfair advantages. You should see the way a negro ovary responds to pituitary! It's quite astonishing, when you're used to working with European material. Still,' he added, with a laugh (but the light of combat was in his eyes and the lift of his chin was challenging), 'still, we mean to beat them if we can. I'm working on a wonderful Delta-Minus ovary at this moment. Only just eighteen months old. Over twelve thousand seven hundred children already, either decanted or in embryo. And still going strong. We'll beat them yet.'

'That's the spirit I like!' cried the Director, and clapped Mr. Foster on the shoulder. 'Come along with us and give these boys the benefit of your expert knowledge.'

Mr. Foster smiled modestly. 'With pleasure.' They went.

In the Bottling Room all was harmonious bustle and ordered activity. Flaps of fresh sow's peritoneum ready cut to the proper size came shooting up in little lifts from the Organ Store in the sub-basement. Whizz and then, click! The lift-hatches flew open; the Bottle-Liner had only to reach out a hand, take the flap, insert, smooth-down, and before the lined bottle had had time to travel out of reach along the endless band, whizz, click! Another flap of peritoneum had shot up from the depths, ready to be slipped into yet another bottle, the next of that slow interminable procession on the band.

Next to the Liners stood the Matriculators. The procession advanced; one by one the eggs were transferred from their test-tubes to the larger containers; deftly the peritoneal lining was slit, the morula dropped into place, the saline solution poured in ... and already the bottle had passed, and it was the turn of the labellers. Heredity, date of fertilization, membership of Bokanovsky Group – details were transferred from test-tube to bottle. No longer anonymous, but named, identified, the procession marched slowly on; on through an opening in the wall, slowly on into the Social Predestination Room.

'Eighty-eight cubic metres of card-index,' said Mr. Foster with relish, as they entered.

'Containing all the relevant information,' added the Director. 'Brought up to date every morning.'

'And co-ordinated every afternoon.'

'On the basis of which they make their calculations.'

'So many individuals, of such and such quality,' said Mr. Foster. 'Distributed in such and such quantities.'

'The optimum Decanting Rate at any given moment.'

'Unforeseen wastages promptly made good.'

'Promptly,' repeated Mr. Foster. 'If you knew the amount of overtime I had to put in after the last Japanese earthquake!' He laughed good-humouredly and shook his head.

'The Predestinators send in their figures to the Fertilizers.'

'Who give them the embryos they ask for.'

'And the bottles come in here to be predestinated in detail.'

'After which they are sent down to the Embryo Store.'

'Where we now proceed ourselves.'

And opening a door Mr. Foster led the way down a staircase into the basement.

The temperature was still tropical. They descended into a thickening twilight. Two doors and a passage with a double turn insured the cellar against any possible infiltration of the day.

'Embryos are like photograph film,' said Mr. Foster waggishly, as he pushed open the second door. 'They can only stand red light.'

And in effect the sultry darkness into which the students now followed him was visible and crimson, like the darkness of closed eyes on a summer's afternoon. The bulging flanks of row on receding row and tier above tier of bottles glinted with innumerable rubies, and among the rubies moved the dim red spectres of men and women with purple eyes and all the symptoms of lupus. The hum and rattle of machinery faintly stirred the air.

'Give them a few figures, Mr. Foster,' said the Director, who was tired of talking.

Mr. Foster was only too happy to give them a few figures.

Two hundred and twenty metres long, two hundred wide, ten high. He pointed upwards. Like chickens drinking, the students lifted their eyes towards the distant ceiling.

Three tiers of racks: ground-floor level, first gallery, second gallery.

The spidery steelwork of gallery above gallery faded away in all directions into the dark. Near them three red ghosts were busily unloading demijohns from a moving staircase.

The escalator from the Social Predestination Room.

Each bottle could be placed on one of fifteen racks, each rack, though you couldn't see it, was a conveyor travelling at the rate of thirty-three and a third centimetres an hour. Two hundred and sixty-seven days at eight metres a day. Two thousand one hundred and thirty-six metres in all. One circuit of the cellar at ground level, one on the first gallery, half

---

The **"Predestinators"** are technicians who decide on the future lives of human beings, for instance, by partly destroying or "conditioning" their embryos.

***to proceed** to move forward, continue

***twilight** *Zwielicht*

infiltration passing through, gradual penetration

waggishly jokingly

sultry hot and humid

bulging protruding, projecting

tier row

***ruby** red jewel

spectre spirit, unnatural apparition, phantom

lupus disease characterized by red patches on the skin

demijohns bottles with narrow necks

conveyor *Förderband*

Two hundred and sixty-seven days the average pregnancy duration

on the second, and on the two hundred and sixty-seventh morning, daylight in the Decanting Room. Independent existence – so called.

'But in the interval,' Mr. Foster concluded, 'we've managed to do a lot to them. Oh, a very great deal.' His laugh was knowing and triumphant.

'That's the spirit I like,' said the Director once more. 'Let's walk round. You tell them everything, Mr. Foster.'

Mr. Foster duly told them.

Told them of the growing embryo on its bed of peritoneum. Made them taste the rich blood surrogate on which it fed. Explained why it had to be stimulated with placentin and thyroxin. Told them of the corpus luteum extract. Showed them the jets through which at every twelfth metre from zero to 2040 it was automatically injected. Spoke of those gradually increasing doses of pituitary administered during the final ninety-six metres of their course. Described the artificial maternal circulation installed on every bottle at metres 112; showed them the reservoir of blood-surrogate, the centrifugal pump that kept the liquid moving over the placenta and drove it through the synthetic lung and waste-product filter. Referred to the embryo's troublesome tendency to anaemia, to the massive doses of hog's stomach extract and foetal foal's liver with which, in consequence, it had to be supplied. Showed them the simple mechanism by means of which, during the last two metres out of every eight, all the embryos were simultaneously shaken into familiarity with movement. Hinted at the gravity of the so-called 'trauma of decanting,' and enumerated the precautions taken to minimize, by a suitable training of the bottled embryo, that dangerous shock. Told them of the tests for sex carried out in the neighbourhood of metre 200. Explained the system of labelling – a T for the males, a circle for the females and for those who were destined to become freemartins a question mark, black on a white ground. 'For of course,' said Mr. Foster, 'in the vast majority of cases, fertility is merely a nuisance. One fertile ovary in twelve hundred – that would really be quite sufficient for our purposes. But we want to have a good choice. And of course one must always leave an enormous margin of safety. So we allow as many as thirty per cent of the female embryos to develop normally. The others get a dose of male sex-hormone every twenty-four metres for the rest of the course. Result: they're decanted as freemartins – structurally quite normal (except,' he had to admit, 'that they do have just the slightest tendency to grow beards), but sterile. Guar-

duly properly, rightfully

surrogate substitute

placentin author-coined word: from placenta: organ that forms on the walls of the uterus and during pregnancy carries nourishment to a growing foetus

thyroxin *Schilddrüsenhormon*
corpus luteum *Gelbkörper;* cell mass that forms in the ovary *(Eierstock)* after the release of an egg

anaemia condition caused by a lack of red blood cells
hog domesticated pig

trauma of decanting The "trauma of birth" or "birth trauma" refers to possible physical or emotional injuries an infant might suffer during or soon after its delivery.
T an allusion to Ford's T-Model (often called "Tin Lizzie"), generally regarded as the first affordable automobile, the car which "put America on wheels" due to assembly line production instead of individual hand crafting.

freemartins here: sterile females
★**nuisance** something annoying
margin here: *Spielraum*

anteed sterile. Which brings us at last,' continued Mr. Foster, 'out of the realm of mere slavish imitation of nature into the much more interesting world of human invention.'

He rubbed his hands. For, of course, they didn't content themselves with merely hatching out embryos: any cow could do that.

'We also predestine and condition. We decant our babies as socialized human beings, as Alphas or Epsilons, as future sewage workers or future...' He was going to say 'future World Controllers,' but correcting himself, said 'future Directors of Hatcheries' instead.

The D.H.C. acknowledged the compliment with a smile.

They were passing metre 320 on rack eleven. A young Beta-Minus mechanic was busy with screw-driver and spanner on the blood-surrogate pump of a passing bottle. The hum of the electric motor deepened by fractions of a tone as he turned the nuts. Down, down... A final twist, a glance at the revolution counter, and he was done. He moved two paces down the line and began the same process on the next pump.

'Reducing the number of revolutions per minute,' Mr. Foster explained. 'The surrogate goes round slower; therefore passes through the lung at longer intervals; therefore gives the embryo less oxygen. Nothing like oxygen-shortage for keeping an embryo below par.' Again he rubbed his hands.

'But why do you want to keep the embryo below par?' asked an ingenuous student.

'Ass!' said the Director, breaking a long silence. 'Hasn't it occurred to you that an Epsilon embryo must have an Epsilon environment as well as an Epsilon heredity?'

It evidently hadn't occurred to him. He was covered with confusion.

'The lower the caste,' said Mr. Foster, 'the shorter the oxygen.' The first organ affected was the brain. After that the skeleton. At seventy per cent of normal oxygen you got dwarfs. At less than seventy, eyeless monsters.

'Who are no use at all,' concluded Mr. Foster.

Whereas (his voice became confidential and eager), if they could discover a technique for shortening the period of maturation what a triumph, what a benefaction to Society!

'Consider the horse.'

They considered it.

Mature at six; the elephant at ten. While at thirteen a man is not yet sexually mature; and is only full grown at twenty. Hence, of course, that fruit of delayed development, the human intelligence.

★**realm** kingdom, domain, area

sewage waste water

nut here: hexagonal metal piece which fastens onto a screw
revolution here: full turn, circuit

below par less than average

ingenuous innocent, naïve

➊ How are Epsilons "produced"?

★**ass** donkey, here: stupid person

★**caste** particularly in Hindu society: class, social position

maturation process of growing up
benefaction benefit, gift

'But in Epsilons,' said Mr. Foster very justly, 'we don't need human intelligence.'

Didn't need and didn't get it. But though the Epsilon mind was mature at ten, the Epsilon body was not fit to work till eighteen. Long years of superfluous and wasted immaturity. If the physical development could be speeded up till it was as quick, say, as a cow's, what an enormous saving to the Community! 'Enormous!' murmured the students. Mr. Foster's enthusiasm was infectious.

He became rather technical; spoke of the abnormal endocrine co-ordination which made men grow so slowly; postulated a germinal mutation to account for it. Could the effects of this germinal mutation be undone? Could the individual Epsilon embryo be made to revert, by a suitable technique, to the normality of dogs and cows? That was the problem. And it was all but solved.

Pilkington, at Mombasa, had produced individuals who were sexually mature at four and full grown at six and a half. A scientific triumph. But socially useless. Six-year-old men and women were too stupid to do even Epsilon work. And the process was an all-or-nothing one; either you failed to modify at all, or else you modified the whole way. They were still trying to find the ideal compromise between adults of twenty and adults of six. So far without success. Mr. Foster sighed and shook his head.

Their wanderings through the crimson twilight had brought them to the neighbourhood of Metre 170 on Rack 9. From this point onwards Rack 9 was enclosed and the bottles performed the remainder of their journey in a kind of tunnel, interrupted here and there by openings two or three metres wide.

'Heat conditioning,' said Mr. Foster.

Hot tunnels alternated with cool tunnels. Coolness was wedded to discomfort in the form of hard X-rays. By the time they were decanted the embryos had a horror of cold. They were predestined to emigrate to the tropics, to be miners and acetate silk spinners and steel workers. Later on their minds would be made to endorse the judgment of their bodies. 'We condition them to thrive on heat,' concluded Mr. Foster. 'Our colleagues upstairs will teach them to love it.'

'And that,' put in the Director sententiously, 'that is the secret of happiness and virtue – liking what you've got to do. All conditioning aims at that: making people like their inescapable social destiny.'

In a gap between two tunnels, a nurse was delicately probing with a long fine syringe into the gelatinous contents of a

---

superfluous more than needed

endocrine internal hormonal secretion

mutation alteration in the genetic constitution

to revert to return to its previous condition

to modify to change, adjust, adapt

What is the aim of "Heat conditioning"?

to be wedded here: to be blended, united

to endorse to approve, sanction

to thrive to prosper, flourish, succeed

What is the secret of happiness in the Brave New World?

sententiously clearly and briefly, with a few well-chosen words

passing bottle. The students and their guides stood watching her for a few moments in silence.

'Well, Lenina,' said Mr. Foster, when at last she withdrew the syringe and straightened herself up.

The girl turned with a start. One could see that, for all the lupus and the purple eyes, she was uncommonly pretty.

'Henry!' Her smile flashed redly at him – a row of coral teeth.

'Charming, charming,' murmured the Director and, giving her two or three little pats, received in exchange a rather deferential smile for himself.

'What are you giving them?' asked Mr. Foster, making his tone very professional.

'Oh, the usual typhoid and sleeping sickness.'

'Tropical workers start being inoculated at metre 150,' Mr. Foster explained to the students. 'The embryos still have gills. We immunize the fish against the future man's diseases.' Then, turning back to Lenina, 'Ten to five on the roof this afternoon,' he said, 'as usual.'

'Charming,' said the Director once more, and, with a final pat, moved away after the others.

On Rack 10 rows of next generation's chemical workers were being trained in the toleration of lead, caustic soda, tar, chlorine. The first of a batch of two hundred and fifty embryonic rocket-plane engineers was just passing the eleven hundredth metre mark on Rack 3. A special mechanism kept their containers in constant rotation. 'To improve their sense of balance,' Mr. Foster explained. 'Doing repairs on the outside of a rocket in mid-air is a ticklish job. We slacken off the circulation when they're right way up, so that they're half starved, and double the flow of surrogate when they're upside down. They learn to associate topsy-turvydom with well-being; in fact, they're only truly happy when they're standing on their heads.' [...]

deferential respectful

typhoid *Typhus*

to be inoculated to be vaccinated, immunized

gill breathing organ of fish

caustic *ätzend*

ticklish requiring special care and handling

to slacken off to slow down, make less intense

topsy-turvydom state of extreme confusion or disorder

Freedom is slavery

George Orwell: 1984

George Orwell (1903–1950), whose real name was Eric Blair, was born in India. After spending his school life at Eaton in England, he went to Burma, where he worked as a policeman and wrote his first novel. Disgusted by his first-hand experience of imperialism, he soon quit and from then on lived in Paris and London. Political idealism led him to fight on the Republican side in the

George Orwell

Spanish Civil War. Orwell's contempt for the police states he saw developing in Spain, Italy, Germany and Russia finally led him to write his two most famous books, *1984*, written in 1948, and *Animal Farm*, written in 1945, a brilliant fable of the success, betrayal and ultimate failure of the Russian Revolution.
The following extract is the beginning of the novel.

It was a bright cold day in April, and the clocks were striking thirteen. Winston Smith, his chin nuzzled into his breast in an effort to escape the vile wind, slipped quickly through the glass doors of Victory Mansions, though not quickly enough to prevent a swirl of gritty dust from entering along with him.

The hallway smelt of boiled cabbage and old rag mats. At one end of it a coloured poster, too large for indoor display, had been tacked to the wall. It depicted simply an enormous face, more than a metre wide: the face of a man of about forty-five, with a heavy black moustache and ruggedly handsome features. Winston made for the stairs. It was no use trying the lift. Even at the best of times it was seldom working, and at present the electric current was cut off during daylight hours. It was part of the economy drive in preparation for Hate Week.

The flat was seven flights up, and Winston, who was thirty-nine and had a varicose ulcer above his right ankle, went slowly, resting several times on the way. On each landing, opposite the lift-shaft, the poster with the enormous face gazed from the wall.

It was one of those pictures which are so contrived that the eyes follow you about when you move. BIG BROTHER IS WATCHING YOU, the caption beneath it ran.

Inside the flat a fruity voice was reading out a list of figures which had something to do with the production of pig-iron. The voice came from an oblong metal plaque like a dulled mirror which formed part of the surface of the right-hand wall. Winston turned a switch and the voice sank somewhat, though the words were still distinguishable. The instrument (the telescreen, it was called) could be dimmed, but there was no way of shutting it off completely. He moved over to the window: a smallish, frail figure, the meagreness of his body merely emphasized by the blue overalls which were the uniform of the party. His hair was very fair, his face naturally sanguine, his skin roughened by coarse soap and blunt razor blades and the cold of the winter that had just ended.

Outside, even through the shut window-pane, the world looked cold. Down in the street little eddies of wind were

to nuzzle to snuggle, nestle
vile filthy, repulsive
***mansion** large and stately home
gritty sandy, grainy
rag piece of old and often torn cloth
to depict to portray, show
ruggedly roughly
***feature** facial structure
varicose swollen, enlarged
ulcer *Geschwür*
contrived intended, devised
pig-iron raw iron
oblong rectangular
dulled without shine
***frail** fragile, weak
sanguine having a reddish complexion
eddy small circular current

whirling dust and torn paper into spirals, and though the sun was shining and the sky a harsh blue, there seemed to be no colour in anything, except the posters that were plastered everywhere. The black-moustachio'd face gazed down from every commanding corner. There was one on the house-front immediately opposite. BIG BROTHER IS WATCHING YOU, the caption said, while the dark eyes looked deep into Winston's own. Down at street level another poster, torn at one corner, flapped fitfully in the wind, alternately covering and uncovering the single word INGSOC. In the far distance a helicopter skimmed down between the roofs, hovered for an instant like a bluebottle, and darted away again with a curving flight. It was the police patrol, snooping into people's windows. The patrols did not matter, however. Only the Thought Police mattered.

Behind Winston's back the voice from the telescreen was still babbling away about pig-iron and the overfulfillment of the Ninth Three-Year Plan. The telescreen received and transmitted simultaneously. Any sound that Winston made, above the level of a very low whisper, would be picked up by it, moreover, so long as he remained within the field of vision which the metal plaque commanded, he could be seen as well as heard. There was of course no way of knowing whether you were being watched at any given moment. How often, or on what system, the Thought Police plugged in on any individual wire was guesswork. It was even conceivable that they watched everybody all the time. But at any rate they could plug in your wire whenever they wanted to. You had to live – did live, from habit that became instinct – in the assumption that every sound you made was overheard, and, except in darkness, every movement scrutinized.

Winston kept his back turned to the telescreen. It was safer, though, as he well knew, even a back can be revealing. A kilometre away the Ministry of Truth, his place of work, towered vast and white above the grimy landscape. This, he thought with a sort of vague distaste – this was London, chief city of Airstrip One, itself the third most populous of the provinces of Oceania. He tried to squeeze out some childhood memory that should tell him whether London had always been quite like this. Were there always these vistas of rotting nineteenth-century houses, their sides shored up with baulks of timber, their windows patched with cardboard and their roofs with corrugated iron, their crazy garden walls sagging in all directions? And the bombed sites where the plaster dust swirled in the air and the willow-herb straggled over the heaps of rub-

INGSOC name of the ruling party, the English Socialists

bluebottle *Schmeißfliege*

➔ What are the two functions of the "telescreen"?

★**conceivable** imaginable

to be scrutinized to be checked closely, examined

grimy dirty, filthy

shored up supported
baulk beam
patched here: covered, repaired
corrugated iron *Wellblech*
to sag to droop, fall inwards
willow-herb *Fuchsie*

ble; and the places where the bombs had cleared a larger patch and there had sprung up sordid colonies of wooden dwellings like chicken-houses? But it was no use, he could not remember: nothing remained of his childhood except a series of bright-lit tableaux occurring against no background and mostly unintelligible.

The Ministry of Truth – Minitrue, in Newspeak – was startlingly different from any other object in sight. It was an enormous pyramidal structure of glittering white concrete, soaring up, terrace after terrace, 300 metres into the air. From where Winston stood it was just possible to read, picked out on its white face in elegant lettering, the three slogans of the Party:

WAR IS PEACE

FREEDOM IS SLAVERY

IGNORANCE IS STRENGTH

The Ministry of Truth contained, it was said, three thousand rooms above ground level, and corresponding ramifications below. Scattered about London there were just three other buildings of similar appearance and size. So completely did they dwarf the surrounding architecture that from the roof of Victory Mansions you could see all four of them simultaneously. They were the homes of the four Ministries between which the entire apparatus of government was divided. The Ministry of Truth, which concerned itself with news, entertainment, education, and the fine arts. The Ministry of Peace, which concerned itself with war. The Ministry of Love, which maintained law and order. And the Ministry of Plenty, which was responsible for economic affairs. Their names, in Newspeak: Minitrue, Minipax, Miniluv, and Miniplenty.

The Ministry of Love was the really frightening one. There were no windows in it at all. Winston had never been inside the Ministry of Love, nor within half a kilometre of it. It was a place impossible to enter except on official business, and then only by penetrating through a maze of barbed-wire entanglements, steel doors, and hidden machine-gun nests. Even the streets leading up to its outer barriers were roamed by gorilla-faced guards in black uniforms, armed with jointed truncheons.

sordid run-down, dirty

tableaux (pl) pictures

unintelligible not comprehensible, not understandable

Newspeak author-coined term for the propagandistic new language of Oceania, which serves political purposes by hiding or twisting the truth.

FREEDOM IS SLAVERY
Such an apparently self-contradictory statement, called *paradox,* is normally supposed to grab attention and provoke fresh thought.

ramification *Verästelung*

to dwarf to make sth look small by comparison

to penetrate to enter with force

maze labyrinth

barbed-wire entanglements (pl) *Stacheldrahtverhau, Hindernisse aus Stacheldraht*

truncheon *Schlagstock*

IV. The present

After the catastrophe

Margaret Atwood: The Handmaid's Tale

Margaret Atwood is Canada's most prominent novelist, poet and literary critic. Born in 1939 in Ottawa, Ontario, Canada, she was educated at the University of Toronto, Radcliffe College and Harvard University. Her 1985 tale of a future dystopia in the science fiction novel *The Handmaid's Tale* won the Arthur C. Clarke Award for Science Fiction as well as the Governor General's Award and was adapted for a movie in 1990 by German director Volker Schlöndorff (*The Tin Drum*). Her other books include *The Edible Women* (1969), *Cat's Eye* (1989), *Oryx and Crake* (2003) and the Booker Prize-winning *The Blind Assassin* (2000). In *The Handmaid's Tale,* rightwing fundamentalists set up Gilead, a theocratic dicatorship. Because nuclear and biological warfare has led to declining birth rates, fertile women are selected as potential breeders. Forcefully separated from their families, they are indoctrinated and passed into the possession of Commanders of the secret police.

Margaret Atwood

I don't feel like a nap this afternoon, there's still too much adrenalin. I sit on the window seat, looking out through the semi-sheer of the curtains. White nightgown. The window is as open as it goes, there's a breeze, hot in the sunlight, and the white cloth blows across my face. From the outside I must look like a cocoon, a spook, face enshrouded like this, only the outlines visible, of nose, bandaged mouth, blind eyes. But I like the sensation, the soft cloth brushing my skin. It's like being in a cloud.

They've given me a small electric fan, which helps in this humidity. It whirs on the floor, in the corner, its blades encased in grillwork. If I were Moira, I'd know how to take it apart, reduce it to its cutting edges. I have no screwdriver, but if I were Moira I could do it without a screwdriver. I'm not Moira.

What would she tell me, about the Commander, if she were here? Probably she'd disapprove. She disapproved of Luke, back then. Not of Luke but of the fact that he was married.

Characterize the narrator from these opening lines (ll. 1–15).

Gilead In Old Testament times, a productive Israelite upland region cast of the Jordan River and northeast of the Death Sea. Gilead was known for its ample flocks of sheep and goats, orchards and vineyards and plentiful spices.
Commander (of the Faithful) – a euphemism for the privileged, authoritarian hierarchy of Gilead

spook ghost
enshrouded concealed, covered
to whir to buzz

★**to poach** to hunt illegally

★**to rationalize** to find reasons to justify incorrect behaviour

scruple uneasy feeling due to bad conscience

even-steven evenly matched

to trivialize to make small or unimportant

carry-over habit continued from the past

clapboard covered with wooden boards

rickety shaky, unstable

cockroach *Schabe*

spider mite *Milbe*

She said I was poaching on another woman's ground. I said Luke wasn't a fish or a piece of dirt either, he was a human being and could make his own decisions. She said I was rationalizing. I said I was in love. She said that was no excuse. Moira was always more logical than I am.

I said she didn't have that problem herself any more, since she'd decided to prefer women, and as far as I could see she had no scruples about stealing them or borrowing them when she felt like it. She said it was different, because the balance of power was equal between women so sex was an even-steven transaction. I said "even-steven" was a sexist phrase, if she was going to be like that, and anyway that argument was out-dated. She said I had trivialized the issue and if I thought it was outdated I was living with my head in the sand.

We said all this in my kitchen, drinking coffee, sitting at my kitchen table, in those low, intense voices we used for such arguments when we were in our early twenties; a carry-over from college. The kitchen was in a run-down apartment in a clapboard house near the river, the kind with three storeys and a rickety outside back staircase. I had the second floor, which meant I got noise from both above and below, two unwanted stereo disc players thumping late into the night. Students, I knew. I was still on my first job, which didn't pay much: I worked a computer in an insurance company. So the hotels, with Luke, didn't mean only love or even only sex to me. They also meant time off from the cockroaches, the dripping sink, the linoleum that was peeling off the floor in patches, even from my own attempts to brighten things up by sticking posters on the wall and hanging prisms in the windows. I had plants, too; though they always got spider mites or died from being unwatered. I would go off with Luke, and neglect them.

I said there was more than one way of living with your head in the sand and that if Moira thought she could create Utopia by shutting herself up in a women-only enclave she was sadly mistaken. Men were not just going to go away, I said. You couldn't just ignore them.

That's like saying you should go out and catch syphilis merely because it exists, Moira said.

Are you calling Luke a social disease? I said.

Moira laughed. Listen to us, she said. Shit. We sound like your mother. We both laughed then, and when she left we hugged each other as usual. There was a time when we didn't hug, after she'd told me about being gay; but then she said I didn't turn her on, reassuring me, and we'd gone back to it.

We could fight and wrangle and name-call, but it didn't change anything underneath. She was still my oldest friend. Is.

I got a better apartment after that, where I lived for the two years it took Luke to pry himself loose. I paid for it myself, with my new job. It was in a library, not the big one with Death and Victory, a smaller one.
I worked transferring books to computer discs, to cut down on storage space and replacement costs, they said. Discers, we called ourselves. We called the library a discotheque, which was a joke of ours. After the books were transferred they were supposed to go to the shredder, but sometimes I took them home with me. I liked the feel of them, and the look. Luke said I had the mind of an antiquarian. He liked that, he liked old things himself.
It's strange, now, to think about having a job. Job. It's a funny word. It's a job for a man. Do a jobbie, they'd say to children, when they were being toilet-trained. Or of dogs: he did a job on the carpet. You were supposed to hit them with rolled-up newspapers, my mother said. I can remember when there were newspapers, though I never had a dog, only cats.
The Book of Job.
All those women having jobs: hard to imagine, now, but thousands of them had jobs, millions. It was considered the normal thing. Now it's like remembering the paper money, when they still had that. My mother kept some of it, pasted into her scrapbook along with the early photos. It was obsolete by then, you couldn't buy anything with it. Pieces of paper, thickish, greasy to the touch, green-coloured, with pictures on each side, some old man in a wig and on the other side a pyramid with an eye above it. It said In God We Trust. My mother said people used to have signs beside their cash registers, for a joke: In God We Trust, All Others Pay Cash. That would be blasphemy now.

You had to take those pieces of paper with you when you went shopping, though by the time I was nine or ten most people used plastic cards. Not for the groceries though, that came later. It seems so primitive, totemistic even, like cowrie shells. I must have used that kind of money myself, a little, before everything went on the Compubank. I guess that's how they were able to do it, in the way they did, all at once, without anyone knowing beforehand. If there had still been portable money, it would have been more difficult.

to pry oneself loose to break free (from his wife)

Death and Victory inscription on the Wall, where the bodies of executed dissidents and former abortionists are displayed

Job biblical figure who suffered many misfortunes, but retained his faith in God

scrapbook blank book for the collection of newspaper clippings, photos etc.

totemistic worshipping a particular animal or plant that is believed to carry the spirit of one's ancestors
cowrie type of sea snail

Compubank author-coined term for computer-based banking

Name the successive steps which were taken to turn a secular Western democracy into a religious dictatorship. Which specific religious and moral issues was the dictatorial overthrow originally intended to protect against? How did the narrator and her environment react to these steps and which reasons are given to justify their behaviour? (see, for example, ll. 1–14; 20–42)

It was after the catastrophe, when they shot the President and machine-gunned the Congress and the army declared a state of emergency. They blamed it on the Islamic fanatics, at the time.

Keep calm, they said on television. Everything is under control.

I was stunned. Everyone was, I know that. It was hard to believe. The entire government, gone like that. How did they get in, how did it happen?

That was when they suspended the Constitution. They said it would be temporary. There wasn't even any rioting in the streets. People stayed home at night, watching television, looking for some direction. There wasn't even an enemy you could put your finger on.

Look out, said Moira to me, over the phone. Here it comes.

Here what comes? I said.

You wait, she said. They've been building up to this. It's you and me up against the wall, baby. She was quoting an expression of my mother's, but she wasn't intending to be funny.

Things continued in that state of suspended animation for weeks, although some things did happen. Newspapers were censored and some were closed down, for security reasons they said. The roadblocks began to appear, and Identipasses. Everyone approved of that, since it was obvious you couldn't be too careful. They said that new elections would be held, but that it would take some time to prepare for them. The thing to do, they said, was to continue on as usual.

The Pornomarts were shut, though, and there were no longer any Feels on Wheels vans and Bun-Die Buggies circling the Square. But I wasn't sad to see them go. We all knew what a nuisance they'd been.

It's high time somebody did something, said the woman behind the counter, at the store where I usually bought my cigarettes. It was on the corner, a newsstand chain: papers, candy, cigarettes. The woman was older, with grey hair; my mother's generation.

Did they just close them, or what? I asked.

She shrugged. Who knows, who cares, she said. Maybe they just moved them off somewhere else. Trying to get rid of it altogether is like trying to stamp out mice, you know? She punched my Compunumber into the till, barely looking at it: I was a regular, by then. People were complaining, she said.

The next morning, on my way to the library for the day, I stopped by the same store for another pack, because I'd run out. I was smoking more those days, it was the tension, you

*__animation__ vitality, wakefulness

Identipasses author-coined term for in-town visas; an unconstitutional restriction on personal freedom
Pornomarts distributors of pornography
Feels on Wheels vans, Bun-Die Buggies vehicles carrying prostitution to the streets

Compunumber a credit registration number, a means by which the religious right controls Gilead's citizens

could feel it, like a subterranean hum, although things seemed so quiet. I was drinking more coffee too, and having trouble sleeping. Everyone was a little jumpy. There was a lot more music on the radio than usual, and fewer words. It was after we'd been married, for years it seemed; she was three or four, in daycare.

We'd all got up in the usual way and had breakfast, granola, I remember, and Luke had driven her off to school, in the little outfit I'd bought her just a couple of weeks before, striped overalls and a blue T-shirt. What month was this? It must have been September. There was a School Pool that was supposed to pick them up, but for some reason I'd wanted Luke to do it, I was getting worried even about the School Pool. No children walked to school any more, there had been too many disappearances.

When I got to the corner store, the usual woman wasn't there. Instead there was a man, a young man, he couldn't have been more than twenty. She sick? I said as I handed him my card.

Who? he said, aggressively I thought.

The woman who's usually here, I said.

How would I know, he said. He was punching my number in, studying each number, punching with one finger. He obviously hadn't done it before. I drummed my fingers on the counter, impatient for a cigarette, wondering if anyone had ever told him something could be done about those pimples on his neck. I remember quite clearly what he looked like: tall, slightly stooped, dark hair cut short, brown eyes that seemed to focus two inches behind the bridge of my nose, and that acne. I suppose I remember him so clearly because of what he said next.

Sorry, he said. This number's not valid.

That's ridiculous, I said. It must be, I've got thousands in my account. I just got the statement two days ago. Try it again.

It's not valid, he repeated obstinately. See that red light? Means it's not valid.

You must have made a mistake, I said. Try it again.

He shrugged and gave me a fed-up smile, but he did try the number again. This time I watched his fingers, on each number, and checked the numbers that came up in the window. It was my number all right, but there was the red light again.

See? he said again, still with that smile, as if he knew some private joke he wasn't going to tell me.

I'll phone them from the office, I said. The system had fouled up before, but a few phone calls usually straightened it out.

subterranean beneath the surface of the Earth, secret

jumpy nervous, tense

granola *Müsli*

statement here: *Bankauszug*

Still, I was angry, as if I'd been unjustly accused of something I didn't even know about. As if I'd made the mistake myself. You do that, he said indifferently. I left the cigarettes on the counter, since I hadn't paid for them. I figured I could borrow some at work.

I did phone from the office, but all I got was a recording. The lines were overloaded, the recording said. Could I please phone back? The lines stayed overloaded all morning, as far as I could tell. I phoned back several times, but no luck. Even that wasn't too unusual. About two o'clock, after lunch, the director came in to the discing room.

I have something to tell you, he said. He looked terrible; his hair was untidy, his eyes were pink and wobbling, as though he'd been drinking. We all looked up, turned off our machines. There must have been eight or ten of us in the room.

wobbling moving from side to side, trembling

I'm sorry, he said, but it's the law. I really am sorry.

For what? somebody said.

I have to let you go, he said. It's the law, I have to. I have to let you all go. He said this almost gently, as if we were wild animals, frogs he'd caught, in a jar, as if he were being humane.

We're being fired? I said. I stood up. But why?

Not fired, he said. Let go. You can't work here any more, it's the law. He ran his hands through his hair and I thought, he's gone crazy. The strain has been too much for him and he's blown his wiring.

to blow one's wiring to go mad

You can't just do that, said the woman who sat next to me. This sounded false, improbable, like something you would say on television. It isn't me, he said. You don't understand. Please go, now. His voice was rising. I don't want any trouble. If there's trouble the books might be lost, things will get broken ... He looked over his shoulder. They're outside, he said, in my office. If you don't go now they'll come in themselves. They gave me ten minutes. By now he sounded crazier than ever.

He's loopy, someone said out loud; which we must all have thought. But I could see out into the corridor, and there were two men standing there, in uniforms, with machine guns. This was too theatrical to be true, yet here they were: sudden apparitions, like Martians. There was a dreamlike quality to them; they were too vivid, too at odds with their surroundings.

loopy confused, drunk, crazy

*** apparition** ghost
at odds out of place

Just leave the machines, he said while we were getting our things together, filing out. As if we could have taken them.

We stood in a cluster, on the steps outside the library. We didn't know what to say to one another. Since none of us understood what had happened, there was nothing much we could say. We looked at one another's faces and saw dismay, and a certain shame, as if we'd been caught doing something we shouldn't.

It's outrageous, one woman said, but without belief. What was it about this that made us feel we deserved it?

cluster group

dismay fear, horror

When I got back to the house nobody was there. Luke was still at work, my daughter was at school. I felt tired, bone-tired, but when I sat down I got up again, I couldn't seem to sit still. I wandered through the house, from room to room. I remember touching things, not even that consciously, just placing my fingers on them; things like the toaster, the sugar bowl, the ashtray in the living room. After a while I picked up the cat and carried her around with me. I wanted Luke to come home. I thought I should do something, take steps; but I didn't know what steps I could take.

The narrator has a very different personality from her friend Moira, especially when facing conflict. Describe these differences.

I tried phoning the bank again, but I only got the same recording. I poured myself a glass of milk – I told myself I was too jittery for another coffee – and went into the living room and sat down on the sofa and put the glass of milk on the coffee table, carefully, without drinking any of it. I held the cat up against my chest so I could feel her purring against my throat.

jittery fidgety, nervous, tense

After a while I phoned my mother at her apartment, but there was no answer. She'd settled down more by then, she'd stopped moving every few years; she lived across the river, in Boston. I waited a while and phoned Moira. She wasn't there either, but when I tried half an hour later she was in. In between those phone calls I just sat on the sofa. What I thought about was my daughter's school lunches. I thought maybe I'd been giving her too many peanut-butter sandwiches.

I've been fired, I told Moira when I got her on the phone. She said she would come over. By that time she was working for a women's collective, the publishing division. They put out books on birth control and rape and things like that, though there wasn't as much demand for those things as there used to be.

collective cooperative enterprise

I'll come over, she said. She must have been able to tell from my voice that this was what I wanted.

She got there after some time. So, she said. She threw off her jacket, sprawled into the oversized chair. Tell me. First we'll have a drink. She got up and went to the kitchen and poured

us a couple of Scotches, and came back and sat down and I tried to tell her what had happened to me. When I'd finished, she said, Tried getting anything on your Compucard today?
Yes, I said. I told her about that too.
They've frozen them, she said. Mine too. The collective's too. Any account with an F on it instead of an M. All they needed to do is push a few buttons. We're cut off.

F, M letters denoting the gender of cardholders

But I've got over two thousand dollars in the bank, I said, as if my own account was the only one that mattered.
Women can't hold property any more, she said. It's a new law. Turned on the TV today?
No, I said.
It's on there, she said. All over the place. She was not stunned, the way I was. In some strange way she was gleeful, as if this was what she'd been expecting for some time and now she'd been proven right. She even looked more energetic, more determined. Luke can use your Compucount for you, she said. They'll transfer your number to him, or that's what they say. Husband or male next of kin.

***gleeful** *hämisch, schadenfroh*

But what about you? I said. She didn't have anyone.
I'll go underground, she said. Some of the gays can take over our numbers and buy us things we need.
But why? I said. Why did they?
Ours is not to reason why, said Moira. They had to do it that way, the Compucounts and the jobs both at once. Can you picture the airports, otherwise? They don't want us going anywhere, you can bet on that.

Ours is not to reason why a paraphrase of a line from Rudyard Kipling's *The Charge of the Light Brigade*, a poem describing the pointless deaths of soldiers dispatched into battle against impossible odds

What role did the confiscation and transfer of property play in the shift of power between the female narrator and her husband Luke, and why?

I went to pick my daughter up from school. I drove with exaggerated care. By the time Luke got home I was sitting at the kitchen table. She was drawing with little felt pens at her own little table in the corner, where her paintings were taped up next to the refrigerator.
Luke knelt beside me and put his arms around me. I heard, he said, on the car radio, driving home. Don't worry, I'm sure it's temporary.
Did they say why? I said.
He didn't answer that. We'll get through it, he said, hugging me.
You don't know what it's like, I said. I feel as if somebody cut off my feet. I wasn't crying. Also, I couldn't put my arms around him.
It's only a job, he said, trying to soothe me.
I guess you get all my money, I said. And I'm not even dead. I was trying for a joke, but it came out sounding macabre.

Hush, he said. He was still kneeling on the floor. You know I'll always take care of you.

I thought, already he's starting to patronize me. Then I thought, already you're starting to get paranoid.

I know, I said. I love you.

Later, after she was in bed and we were having supper, and I wasn't feeling so shaky, I told him about the afternoon. I described the director coming in, blurting out his announcement. It would have been funny if it wasn't so awful, I said. I thought he was drunk. Maybe he was. The army was there, and everything.

Then I remembered something I'd seen and hadn't noticed, at the time. It wasn't the army. It was some other army.

There were marches, of course, a lot of women and some men. But they were smaller than you might have thought. I guess people were scared. And when it was known that the police, or the army, or whoever they were, would open fire almost as soon as any of the marches even started, the marches stopped. A few things were blown up, post offices, subway stations. But you couldn't even be sure who was doing it. It could have been the army, to justify the computer searches and the other ones, the door-to-doors.

I didn't go on any of the marches. Luke said it would be futile and I had to think about them, my family, him and her. I did think about my family. I started doing more housework, more baking. I tried not to cry at mealtimes. By this time I'd started to cry, without warning, and to sit beside the bedroom window, staring out. I didn't know many of the neighbours, and when we met, outside on the street, we were careful to exchange nothing more than the ordinary greetings. Nobody wanted to be reported, for disloyalty.

*futile fruitless, unproductive

Remembering this, I remember also my mother, years before. I must have been fourteen, fifteen, that age when daughters are most embarrassed by their mothers. I remember her coming back to one of our many apartments, with a group of other women, part of her ever-changing circle of friends. They'd been in a march that day; it was during the time of the porn riots, or was it the abortion riots, they were close together. There were a lot of bombings then: clinics, video stores; it was hard to keep track.

The narrator not only has a very different personality from her friend Moira, but also from her mother. Give examples from p. 49, l. 32–p. 50, l. 15.

My mother had a bruise on her face, and a little blood. You can't stick your hand through a glass window without getting cut, is what she said about it. Fucking pigs.

pigs here: police

Fucking bleeders, one of her friends said. They called the other side bleeders, after the signs they carried: Let them bleed. So it must have been the abortion riots.

I went into my bedroom, to be out of their way. They were talking too much, and too loudly. They ignored me, and I resented them. My mother and her rowdy friends. I didn't see why she had to dress that way, in overalls, as if she were young; or to swear so much.

You're such a prude, she would say to me, in a tone of voice that was on the whole pleased. She liked being more outrageous than I was, more rebellious. Adolescents are always such prudes.

Part of my disapproval was that, I'm sure: perfunctory, routine. But also I wanted from her a life more ceremonious, less subject to makeshift and decampment.

You were a wanted child, God knows, she would say at other moments, lingering over the photo albums in which she had me framed; these albums were thick with babies, but my replicas thinned out as I grew older, as if the population of my duplicates had been hit by some plague. She would say this a little regretfully, as though I hadn't turned out entirely as she'd expected. No mother is ever, completely, a child's idea of what a mother should be, and I suppose it works the other way around as well. But despite everything, we didn't do badly by one another, we did as well as most.

I wish she were here, so I could tell her I finally know this.

Someone has come out of the house. I hear the distant closing of a door, around at the side, footsteps on the walk. It's Nick, I can see him now; he's stepped off the path, onto the lawn, to breathe in the humid air which stinks of flowers, of pulpy growth, of pollen thrown into the wind in handfuls, like oyster spawn into the sea. All this prodigal breeding. He stretches in the sun, I feel the ripple of muscles go along him, like a cat's back arching. He's in his shirt sleeves, bare arms sticking shamelessly out from the rolled cloth. Where does the tan end? I haven't spoken to him since that one night, dreamscape in the moon-filled sitting room. He's only my flag, my semaphore. Body language.

Right now his cap's on sideways. Therefore I am sent for.

What does he get for it, his role as page boy? How does he feel, pimping in this ambiguous way for the Commander? Does it fill him with disgust, or make him want more of me, want me more? Because he has no idea what really goes on in there, among the books. Acts of perversion, for all he knows. The Commander and me, covering each other with ink,

★**to resent** to have angry or bitter feelings about

★**prude** self-righteous, conservative person

★**perfunctory** superficial, careless

★**makeshift** *Notbehelf*

decampment act of leaving suddenly

replica duplicate, copy

Characterize the images used in this passage (ll. 27–38). What does Nick signify for the narrator?

Nick is working as a chauffeur in the same house as the first-person narrator, the Handmaid, who also fears that he is an Eye, a police spy. Whereas most of the book deals with the Handmaid's past and is written in the past tense, this passage (ll. 27ff.) is set and written in the present.

prodigal wasteful, abundant

semaphore a coded system of flag movements used at sea for ship-to-ship or ship-to-shore communication

to pimp to manage prostitution

licking it off, or making love on stacks of forbidden newsprint. Well, he wouldn't be far off at that.

But depend on it, there's something in it for him. Everyone's on the take, one way or another. Extra cigarettes? Extra freedoms, not allowed to the general run? Anyway, what can he prove? It's his word against the Commander's, unless he wants to head a posse. Kick in the door, and what did I tell you? Caught in the act, sinfully Scrabbling. Quick, eat those words.

Maybe he just likes the satisfaction of knowing something secret. Of having something on me, as they used to say. It's the kind of power you can use only once.

I would like to think better of him.

stack pile

on the take accepting bribes or illegal income

posse here: military unit mobilized to preserve law and order

That night, after I'd lost my job, Luke wanted me to make love. Why didn't I want to? Desperation alone should have driven me. But I still felt numbed. I could hardly even feel his hands on me.

What's the matter? he said.

I don't know, I said.

We still have ... he said. But he didn't go on to say what we still had. It occurred to me that he shouldn't be saying we, since nothing that I knew of had been taken away from him.

We still have each other, I said. It was true. Then why did I sound, even to myself, so indifferent?

He kissed me then, as if now I'd said that, things could get back to normal. But something had shifted, some balance. I felt shrunken, so that when he put his arms around me, gathering me up, I was small as a doll. I felt love going forward without me.

He doesn't mind this, I thought. He doesn't mind it at all. Maybe he even likes it. We are not each other's, anymore. Instead, I am his. Unworthy, unjust, untrue. But that is what happened.

So Luke: what I want to ask you now, what I need to know is, Was I right? Because we never talked about it. By the time I could have done that, I was afraid too. I couldn't afford to lose you.

Sum up to what extent the relationship between the married couple has changed.

L. and A. Wachowski

It is the world that has been pulled over your eyes to blind you from the truth

Larry and Andy Wachowski: The Matrix

Larry Wachowski (*1965) and Andy Wachowski (*1967) are American film producers, directors and scriptwriters who are most famous for *The Matrix Trilogy*.

"Our films were never intended for a passive audience. There are enough of those kinds of films being made. We wanted our audience to have to work, to have to think, to have to actually participate in order to enjoy them". (http://whatisthematrix.warnerbros.com)

On the future Earth, all appears OK and normal, but to some, things are not right.

One day the film's hero, Neo, is arrested by agents of the state.

INT. abbreviation for interior, inside

INT. INTERROGATION ROOM

CLOSE ON *a camera monitor; wide angle view of a white room where Neo is sitting at a table alone.*

WE MOVE INTO *the Monitor, entering the room as if the monitor was a window.*

manila made of thin cardboard or strong paper

At the same moment, the door opens and the agents enter. Agent Smith sits down across from Neo. A thick manila envelope slaps down on the table between them.

Neo glances at the name on the file: "Anderson, Thomas A."

Why is Neo being interrogated by Agent Smith? By what means does he try to make Neo confess?

AGENT SMITH: As you can see, we've had our eye on you for some time now, Mr. Anderson.

He opens the file. Paper rattle marks the silence as he flips several pages. Neo cannot tell if he is looking at the file or at him.

AGENT SMITH: It seems that you have been living two lives. In one life, you are Thomas A. Anderson, program writer for a respectable software company. You have a social security number, you pay your taxes and you help your landlady carry out her garbage.

The pages continue to turn.

AGENT SMITH: The other life is lived in computers where you go by the hacker alias Neo, and are guilty of virtually every computer crime we have a law for.

Neo feels himself sinking into a pit of shit.

AGENT SMITH: One of these lives has a future. One of them does not.

He closes the file.

*__forthcoming__ candid, open

AGENT SMITH: I'm going to be as forthcoming as I can be, Mr. Anderson. You are here because we need your help.

He removes his sunglasses, his eyes are unnatural ice-blue.

AGENT SMITH: We know that you have been contacted by a certain individual. A man who calls himself Morpheus. Whatever you think you know about this man is irrelevant to the fact that he is wanted for acts of terrorism in more countries than any other man in the world. He is considered by many authorities to be the most dangerous man alive.

He leans closer.

AGENT SMITH: My colleagues believe that I am wasting my time with you but I believe you want to do the right thing. It is obvious that you are an intelligent man, Mr. Anderson, and that you are interested in the future. That is why I believe you are ready to put your past mistakes behind you and get on with your life.

Neo stares to match his stare.

AGENT SMITH: We are willing to wipe the slate clean, to give you a fresh start and all we are asking in return is your cooperation in bringing a known terrorist to justice.

to wipe the slate clean to forget past mistakes

Neo nods to himself.

NEO Yeah. Wow. That sounds like a real good deal. But I think I have a better one. How about I give you the finger –

He does.

NEO: And you can cram that file up your Secret Service sphincter.

sphincter *Schließmuskel*

Agent Smith puts his glasses back on.

AGENT SMITH: You disappoint me, Mr. Anderson.

NEO: You can't scare me with Gestapo crap. I know my rights. I want my phone call!

Agent Smith smiles.

AGENT SMITH: And tell me, Mr. Anderson, what good is a phone call if you are unable to speak?

The question unnerves Neo and strangely he begins to feel the muscles in his jaw tighten. The standing agents snicker, watching Neo's confusion grow into panic. Neo feels his lips grow soft and sticky as they slowly seal shut, melding into each other until all traces of his mouth are gone. Wild with fear, he lunges for the door but the agents restrain him, holding him in the chair.

to snicker to laugh quietly

***to seal** to close

***to meld** to lose shape, blend gradually

***to lunge** to move forward suddenly

AGENT SMITH: You are going to help us, Mr. Anderson, whether you want to or not.

Smith nods and the other two rip open his shirt. From a case taken out of his suit coat, Smith removes a long, fiber-optic wire tap. Neo struggles helplessly as Smith dangles the wire over his exposed abdomen. Horrified, he watches as the electronic device animates, becoming an organic creature that resembles a hybrid

tap plug, stopper

abdomen belly

***hybrid** crossbreed

fluke worm *Saugwurm*
tendrils (pl) threadlike parts of a climbing plant
to probe to examine, explore
to buck to move quickly and violently
umbilical cord cord connecting a developing fetus with the placenta
to thrash to move wildly or violently
to bolt to move suddenly

of an insect and a fluke worm. Thin, whisker-like tendrils reach out and probe into Neo's navel. He bucks wildly as Smith drops the creature which looks for a moment like an uncut umbilical cord – before it begins to burrow, its tail thrashing as it worms its way inside.

INT. NEO'S APARTEMENT

Screaming, Neo bolts upright in bed. He realizes that he is home. Was it a dream ? His mouth is normal. His stomach looks fine. He starts to take a deep, everything-is-okay breath when – the PHONE RINGS.
It almost stops his heart. It continues RINGING, building pressure in the room, forcing him up out of bed, sucking him in with an almost gravitational force. He answers it, saying nothing.

Who is Morpheus? Why does he contact Neo?

tapped *angezapft*
V.O. abbreviation for voice-over, i.e. a character's voice can be heard although he or she is not present

MORPHEUS (V.O.): This line is tapped so I must be brief.
NEO: The agents –
MORPHEUS (V.O.): They got to you first, but they've underestimated how important you are. If they knew what I know, you would probably be dead.
NEO: What do you know?
MORPHEUS (V.O.): You're the One, Neo. You see, you may have spent the last few years looking for me, but I've spent most of my life looking for you.
Neo feels sick.
MORPHEUS (V.O.): Do you still want to meet?
NEO: ... Yes.
MORPHEUS (V.O.): Go to the Adams Street bridge.
CLICK. *He closes his eyes, unsure of what he has done.*

EXT. abbreviation for exterior, outside
to scrape to rub, make a harsh grating noise
★**to slide** to move smoothly, glide

EXT. CITY STREET – NIGHT

It is just beyond the middle of the night; that time when it seems there are no rules and everything feels unsafe. Neo's boots scrape against the concrete. Every pair of eyes he passes seems to follow him. As he reaches the bridge, headlights creep in behind him. He turns just as the car slides quickly to a stop beside him. The back door opens.
TRINITY: Get in.

INT. CAR

★**androgyne** person with male and female characteristics

A large black man named APOC is driving. Beside him is a beautiful androgyne called SWITCH, aiming a large gun at Neo.
NEO: What the hell is this?!
TRINITY: It's necessary, Neo. For our protection.
NEO: From what?
TRINITY: From you.

She lifts a strange steel and glass device that looks like a cross between a rib separator, speculum and air compressor.

separator device to move things apart
speculum medical mirror

Switch: Take off your shirt.

He looks at the strange device and the gun still trained on him.

Neo: What? Why?

Switch: Stop the car.

Apoc does.

Switch: Listen to me, coppertop! We don't have time for 'twenty questions.' Right now there is only one rule. Our way or the highway.

coppertop brownish colour (like copper)

Neo: Fine.

Trinity: No, we can't let him go –

Neo opens the door.

Trinity: Neo, please, you have to trust me.

Neo: Why?

Trinity: Because you've been down there, Neo. You already know that road. You know exactly where it ends.

Neo stares out into the dark street beyond the open door.

Trinity: And I know that's not where you want to be.

Neo: ... shit.

He closes the door.

Ext. Lower Wacker

A moment later the green lights of Lower Wacker curve over the car's tinted windshield as it rushes through the underworld.

Lower Wacker street in Chicago

Int. Car

***tinted** shaded, darkened

Neo grudgingly strips off his T-shirt.

***grudgingly** unwillingly, reluctantly

Trinity: Lie back.

Neo: What is this thing?

Trinity: We think you're bugged. Try to relax.

She turns a dial and the machine bears down on Neo's midsection, the cylinder sucking hard at his stomach.

Neo screams, squinting in pain as Trinity watches the needle on a pressure gauge climb steadily.

***to squint** to look with one's eyes half closed
pressure gauge *Druckmesser*

Trinity: Come on, come on...

The machine quivers as the pressure builds higher and higher until something finally rockets wetly out of Neo's stomach through the machine's coils.

coil cylinder

Trinity: Got it.

Trinity shuts off the compressor, Neo cradling his stomach.

***to cradle** to hold and fondle protectively
spleen *Milz*

Neo: Got what? My spleen?

Trinity lifts a glass cage at the end of the tubing. Inside the small fluke-like bug flips and squirms, its tendrils flapping

fluke *Saugwurm*

against the clear walls. She unrolls the window and dumps it out.

EXT. CAR

tink sharp, quick sound
to revert to return to a previous condition

It hits the pavement with a metallic tink, reverted back into a common wire tap, as the car disappears down the street.

EXT. HOTEL LAFAYETTE

The car stops in a deserted alley behind a forgotten hotel.

INT. LAFAYETTE

***putrefying** decaying, rotten
maggotry area that is full of fly larvae

It is a place of putrefying elegance, a rotting host of urban maggotry.
Trinity leads Neo from the stairwell down the hall of the thirteenth floor. They stop outside room 1313.
TRINTIY: This is it.
Neo can hear his own heart pounding.
TRINTIY: Let me give one piece of advice. Be honest. He knows more than you can possibly imagine.

INT. ROOM 1313

lace *Spitze*

Across the room, a DARK FIGURE *stares out the tall windows veiled with decaying lace. He turns and his smile lights up the room.*
MORPHEUS: At last.
He wears a long black coat and his eyes are invisible behind circular mirrored glasses. He strides to Neo and they shake hands.
MORPHEUS: Welcome, Neo. As you no doubt have guessed, I am Morpheus.
NEO: It's an honor.
MORPHEUS: Please. Come. Sit.
He nods to Trinity.
MORPHEUS: Thank you, Trinity.

adjacent *angrenzend*

She bows her head sharply and exits through a door to an adjacent room. They sit across from one another in cracked, burgundy-leather chairs.

Alice ... hole reference to Lewis Carroll's *Alice in Wonderland;* compare p. 57, ll. 40f. and p. 58, ll. 1f.

MORPHEUS: I imagine, right now, you must be feeling a bit like Alice, tumbling down the rabbit hole?
NEO: You could say that.
MORPHEUS: I can see it in your eyes. You have the look of a man who accepts what he sees because he is expecting to wake up.
A smile, razor-thin, curls the corner of his lips.
MORPHEUS: Ironically, this is not far from the truth. But I'm getting ahead of myself. Can you tell me, Neo, why are you here?

NEO: You're Morpheus, you're a legend. Most hackers would die to meet you.

MORPHEUS: Yes. Thank you. But I think we both know there's more to it than that. Do you believe in fate, Neo?

NEO: No.

MORPHEUS: Why not?

NEO: Because I don't like the idea that I'm not in control of my life.

MORPHEUS: I know exactly what you mean.

Again, that smile that could cut glass.

MORPHEUS: Let me tell you why you are here. You have come because you know something. What you know you can't explain but you feel it. You've felt it your whole life, felt that something is wrong with the world. You don't know what, but it's there like a splinter in your mind, driving you mad. It is this feeling that brought you to me. Do you know what I'm talking about?

NEO: The Matrix?

MORPHEUS: Do you want to know what it is?

Neo swallows hard and nods.

MORPHEUS: The Matrix is everywhere, it's all around us, here even in this room. You can see it out your window or on your television. You feel it when you go to work, or go to church or pay your taxes. It is the world that has been pulled over your eyes to blind you from the truth.

NEO: What truth?

MORPHEUS: That you are a slave, Neo. Like everyone else, you were born into bondage, kept inside a prison that you cannot smell, taste, or touch. A prison for your mind.

*bondage slavery

The LEATHER CREAKS as he leans back.

MORPHEUS: Unfortunately, no one can be told what the Matrix is. You have to see it for yourself.

Morpheus opens his hands. In the right is a red pill. In the left, a blue pill.

Explain the symbolic meaning of the blue and the red pill (ll. 33–45).

MORPHEUS: This is your last chance. After this, there is no going back. You take the blue pill and the story ends. You wake in your bed and you believe whatever you want to believe.

The pills in his open hands are reflected in the glasses.

MORPHEUS: You take the red pill and you stay in Wonderland and I show you how deep the rabbit hole goes.

Neo feels the smooth skin of the capsules, the moisture growing in his palms.

MORPHEUS: Remember that all I am offering is the truth. Nothing more.

Cheshire Cat Character from *Alice in Wonderland* that can vanish so suddenly that its smile remains even after the cat is already gone.

Neo opens his mouth and swallows the red pill. The Cheshire smile returns.

MORPHEUS: Follow me.

He leads Neo into the other room, which is cramped with high-tech equipment, glowing ash-blue and electric green from the racks of monitors. Trinity, Apoc and Cypher look up as they enter.

MORPHEUS: Apoc, are we on-line?

APOC: Almost.

hard-wiring connecting

He and Trinity are working quickly, hard-wiring a complex system of monitors, modules and drives.

MORPHEUS: Neo, time is always against us. Will you take a seat there?

Neo sits in a chair in the center of the room and Trinity begins gently fixing white electrode disks to his head, arms, and the back of his neck. Near the chair is an old oval dressing mirror that is cracked.

He whispers to Trinity:

NEO: You did all this?

She nods, placing a set of headphones over his ears. They are wired to an old hotel phone.

★**to disrupt** to interrupt
★**to pinpoint** to locate exactly
to buckle up to fasten your seatbelt

MORPHEUS: The pill you took is part of a trace program. It's designed to disrupt your input/output carrier signal so we can pinpoint your location.

NEO: What does that mean?

buckle up … Kansas reference to Dorothy, a character from *The Wizard of Oz*

CYPHER: It means buckle up, Dorothy, 'cause Kansas is going bye-bye.

to bead to cover with pearls
to heal here: to repair

Distantly, through the ear phones, he hears Apoc pounding on a keyboard. Sweat beads his face. His eyes blink and twitch when he notices the mirror. Wide-eyed, he stares as it begins to heal itself, a webwork of cracks that slowly run together as though the mirror were becoming liquid.

NEO: Shit...

reams (pl) large amounts of paper
★**rippling** forming small waves
strand string, cord
taffy *Toffee*

Cypher works with Apoc, checking reams of phosphorescent data. Trinity monitors Neo's electric vital signs. Neo reaches out to touch the mirror and his fingers disappear beneath the rippling surface. Quickly, he tries to pull his fingers out but the mirror stretches in long rubbery strands like mirrored-taffy stuck to his fingertips.

MORPHEUS: Have you ever had a dream, Neo, that you were so sure was real?

NEO: This can't be...

MORPHEUS: Be what? Be real?

wisp small bundle of thin material

The strands are thin like rubber cement as he pulls away, until the fragile wisps of mirror thread break.

MORPHEUS: What if you were unable to wake from that dream, Neo? How would you know the difference between the dream world and the real world?

With the TINKLING of GLASS, shimmering SNOWFLAKES of electric-blinking mercury fall, HIT the GROUND, and fade. Neo looks at his hand; fingers distended into mirrored icicles that begin to melt rapidly, dripping, running like wax down his fingers, spreading across his palm where he sees his face reflected.

NEO: Uh-oh...

TRINITY: It's going into replication.

MORPHEUS: Apoc?

APOC: Still nothing.

Morpheus takes out a cellular phone and dials a number.

MORPHEUS: Tank, we're going to need the signal soon.

The mirror gel seems to come to life, racing, crawling up his arms like hundreds of insects.

NEO: It's cold.

The mirror creeps up his neck as Neo begins to panic, tipping his head as though he were sinking into the mirror, trying to keep his mouth up.

NEO: It's all over me –

Morpheus is right next to him with the phone.

TRINITY: I got a fibrillation!

MORPHEUS: Shit! Apoc?

Streams of mercury run from Neo's nose.

APOC: Targeting ... almost there.

An ALARM on Trinity's monitor ERUPTS.

TRINITY: He's going into arrest!

APOC: Lock! I got him!

MORPHEUS: Now, Tank, now!

His eyes tear with mirror, rolling up and closing as a high-pitched ELECTRIC SCREAM erupts in the headphones – It is a piercing shriek like a computer calling to another computer – Neo's body arches in agony and we are PULLED [...] INTO his scream and swallowed by DARKNESS.

INT. POWER PLANT – CLOSE ON MAN'S BODY

floating in a womb-red amnion. His body spasms, fighting against the thick gelatine. Metal tubes, surreal versions of hospital tubes, obscure his face. Other lines like IVs are connected to limbs and cover his genitals. He is struggling desperately now. Air bubbles into the Jell-O but does not break the surface. Pressing up, the surface distends, stretching like a red rubber cocoon. Unable to breathe, he fights wildly to stand, clawing at the thinning elastic shroud –

***mercury** quicksilver

distended bloated, swollen, extended

***replication** duplication, copying

fibrillation involuntary contraction of muscles

arrest *Herzstillstand*

womb *Gebärmutter*

amnion membrane surrounding an embryo

***spasm** cramp

***to obscure** to make indistinct, vague or cloudy

IV abbreviation for intravenous

Jell-O *Wackelpudding*

***shroud** cover, veil

to rupture to tear, burst
slick smooth, slippery
Sum up Neo's experience in the Power Plant.
alloy *Legierung*
curdled sour
★**grafted** joined, implanted
coaxial here: transmission cable
pod here: container
★**core** central part, heart
★**to assault** to attack, shock
murk darkness, gloom
★**abyss** chasm, hell
★**warped** twisted, distorted

Leviathan biblical sea monster (Psalms 74,14)

polymers compound made of many joined monomers (single molecules)
★**to disengage** to disconnect, release
cerebrum *Großhirn*
anterior front
ooze thick messy substance
★**spinal** referring to the backbone
banking here: sloping, slanting, sliding

until it ruptures, a hole widening around his mouth as he sucks for air. Tearing himself free, he emerges from the cell. It is Neo. He is bald and naked, his body slick with gelatine. Dizzy, nauseous, he waits for his vision to focus. He is standing in an oval capsule of clear alloy filled with red gelatine, the surface of which has solidified like curdled milk. The IVs in his arms are plugged into outlets that appear to be grafted to his flesh. He feels the weight of another cable and reaches to the back of his head where he finds an enormous coaxial plugged and locked into the base of his skull. He tries to pull it out but it would be easier to pull off a finger. To either side he sees other tube-shaped pods filled with red gelatine; beneath the wax-like surface, pale and motionless, he sees other human beings. Fanning out in a circle, there are more. All connected to a center core, each capsule like a red, dimly-glowing petal attached to a black metal stem. Above him, level after level, the stem rises seemingly forever. He moves to the foot of the capsule and looks out. The image assaults his mind. Towers of glowing petals spiral up to incomprehensible heights, disappearing down into a dim murk like an underwater abyss. His sight is blurred and warped, exaggerating the intensity of the vision. The sound of the PLANT *is* LIKE *the sound of the* OCEAN *heard from inside the belly of Leviathan. From above, a machine drops directly in front of Neo. He swallows his scream as it seems to stare at him. It is almost insect-like in its design; beautiful housings of alloyed metal covering organic-like systems of hard and soft polymers. The machine seizes hold of Neo, paralyzing him as the cable lock at the back of his neck spins and opens. The cable disengages itself. A long clear plastic needle and cerebrum-chip slides from the anterior of Neo's skull with an ooze of blood and spinal fluid. The other connective hoses snap free and snake away as the machine lets Neo go. Suddenly, the back of the unit opens and a tremendous vacuum, like an airplane door opening, sucks the gelatine and then Neo into a black hole.*

INT. WASTE LINE

The pipe is a waste disposal system and Neo falls, sliding with the clot of gelatine. BANKING THROUGH *pipe spirals and elbows, flushing UP through grease traps clogged with oily clumps of cellulite. Neo begins to drown when he is suddenly snatched from the flow of waste. The metallic cable then lifts, pulling him up into the belly of the futuristic flying machine hovering inside the sewer main.*

INT. HOVERCRAFT

The metal harness opens and drops the half-conscious Neo onto the floor. Human hands and arms help him up as he finds himself looking straight at Morpheus. He smiles.

MORPHEUS: Welcome to the real world, Neo. […] Sit down.

Neo stands at the back of the chair as Morpheus sits.

NEO: Right now, we're inside a computer program?

MORPHEUS: Wild, isn't it?

Neo's hands run over the cracked leather.

NEO: This isn't real?

MORPHEUS: What is real? How do you define real? If you're talking about your senses, what you feel, taste, smell, or see, then all you're talking about are electrical signals interpreted by your brain.

He picks up a remote control and clicks on the television.

On the television, we glide over Lake Michigan towards the glinting skyscrapers of the Windy City skyline circa 1997.

What seems to have happened to the world between the end of the twentieth century and Neo's time?

MORPHEUS: This is the Chicago you know. Chicago as it was at the end of the Twentieth Century. This Chicago exists only as part of a neural-interactive simulation that we call the Matrix.

glinting shining, glittering
Windy City Chicago
★**neural** nerve-related

He changes the channel and we see a very different Chicago as we enter the television.

MORPHEUS: You have been living inside a dreamworld, Neo. As in Baudrillard's vision, your whole life has been spent inside the map, not the territory. This is Chicago as it exists today.

Baudrillard famous French social theorist

In the distance, we see the ruins of a future Chicago protruding from the wasteland like the blackened ribs of a long-dead corpse.

MORPHEUS: The desert of the real.

Beneath us, the lake is gone. We turn and descend, spiraling down toward the lake bed which is scorched and split like burnt flesh, where we find Morpheus and Neo.

MORPHEUS: The average temperature in Chicago these days is minus eighty degrees Celsius. Of course, the wind chill makes it feel like minus one-twenty.

Neo clings to the chair, trying to get his bearings.

bearings orientation

MORPHEUS: We have only bits and pieces of information. What we know for certain is that, at some point in the early Twenty-first Century, all of mankind was united in celebration. Through the blinding inebriation of hubris, we marvelled at our magnificence as we gave birth to A.I.

inebriation drunkenness, intoxication
hubris arrogance

NEO: A.I.? You mean artificial intelligence?

MORPHEUS: Yes. A singular consciousness that spawned an entire race of machines. I must say I find it almost funny to imagine the world slapping itself on the back, toasting the new age. I say almost funny.

to spawn to reproduce, create

obsidian black but transparent
to roil *eintrüben*

to scorch here: to destroy completely

He looks up and his sunglasses reflect the obsidian clouds roiling overhead.

MORPHEUS: We don't know who struck first. Us or them. But we do know it was us that scorched the sky. At the time, they were dependent on solar power. It was believed they would be unable to survive without an energy source as abundant as the sun.

As we descend into the circular window of his glasses, there is a flash of lightning.

MORPHEUS: Throughout human history, we have been dependent on machines to survive. Fate, it seems, is not without a sense of irony.

EXT. FETUS FIELDS

On the flash, we PULL BACK from the darkness which reveals itself to be the black eye of a foetus.

MORPHEUS: The Machines discovered a new form of fusion. All they needed was a small electrical charge to initiate the reaction.

husk outer covering
malleable flexible
brain-jack here: connector

The foetus is suspended in a placenta-like husk, where its malleable skull is already growing around the brain-jack.

B.T.U. abbreviation for British Thermal Unit

MORPHEUS: The human body generates more bioelectricity than a 120-volt battery and over 25,000 B.T.U.'s of body heat.

stalk stem (of a plant)

The husk hanging from a stalk is plucked by a thresher-like farm machine.

***to liquefy** to cause to melt, change into a liquid

MORPHEUS: For the longest time, I wouldn't believe it. But then I saw the fields with my own eyes, spreading in every direction for miles. Inside the power plant, I watched them liquefy the dead so they could be fed intravenously to the living and standing there, facing the efficiency, the pure, horrifying precision, I came to realize the obviousness of the truth.

Still PULLING BACK, we see the image of the field now on the television as we return to the white space of the construct.

INT. CONSTRUCT

Morpheus steps INTO VIEW as he clicks off the television.

MORPHEUS: What is the Matrix? Control.

He opens the back of the television remote control.

MORPHEUS: The Matrix is a computer-generated dreamworld built to keep us under control in order to change a human being into this.

He holds up a coppertop battery.

NEO: No! I don't believe it! It's not possible!
MORPHEUS: I didn't say that it would be easy, Neo. I just said that it would be the truth.

Bonfire

Margaret Atwood: Oryx and Crake

VOICE

"Now I'm alone," he says out loud. "All, all alone. Alone on a wide, wide sea." One more scrap from the burning scrapbook in his head.

Revision: seashore.

He feels the need to hear a human voice – a fully human voice, like his own. Sometimes he laughs like a hyena or roars like a lion – his idea of a hyena, his idea of a lion. He used to watch old DVDs of such creatures when he was a child: those animal-behaviour programs featuring copulation and growling and innards, and mothers licking their young. Why had he found them so reassuring?

Or he grunts and squeals like a pigoon, or howls like a wolvog: *Aroo! Aroo!* Sometimes in the dusk he runs up and down on the sand, flinging stones at the ocean and screaming, *Shit, shit, shit, shit, shit!* He feels better afterwards.

He stands up and raises his arms to stretch, and his sheet falls off. He looks down at his body with dismay: the grimy, bug-bitten skin, the salt-and-pepper tufts of hair, the thickening yellow toenails. Naked as the day he was born, not that he can remember a thing about that. So many crucial events take place behind people's backs, when they aren't in a position to watch: birth and death, for instance. And the temporary oblivion of sex.

"Don't even think about it," he tells himself. Sex is like drink, it's bad to start brooding about it too early in the day.

He used to take good care of himself; he used to run, work out at the gym. Now he can see his own ribs: he's wasting away. Not enough animal protein. A woman's voice says caressingly in his ear, *Nice, buns!* It isn't Oryx, it's some other woman. Oryx is no longer very talkative.

"Say anything," he implores her. She can hear him, he needs to believe that, but she's giving him the silent treatment. "What can I do?" he asks her. "You know I…"

scrap piece, fragment
revision here: correction
to growl to make low, guttural animal sounds
innards bowels, internal organs
grimy dirty, filthy
tuft clump
oblivion state allowing one to forget everything

pigoon author coined-term: At "OrganInc Farms", where Jimmy's father used to work, genetic engineering was carried out. The goal of the "pigoon project" was to grow human organs in a pig host, organs that could easily be transplanted and would be able to fend off attacks by microbes or viruses, of which there were more and more every year. Pigoons could grow six kidneys at a time. The host animal could be reaped of its extra kidneys and would grow new ones. None of the pigoons was supposed to end up "as bacon and sausage: no one would want to eat an animal whose cells might be identical with at least some of their own. Still, as time went on and the coastal aquifers turned salty and the northern permafrost melted and the vast tundra bubbled with methane, and the draft in the midcontinental plains went on and on, and the Asian steppes turned to sand dunes, and meat became harder to come by", […] within OrganInc Farms "it was noticeable how often back bacon and ham sandwiches and pork pies turned up on the staff café menu". (Atwood, Oryx and Crake, p. 27)

Oh, nice abs! comes the whisper, interrupting him. *Honey, just lie back.* Who is it? Some tart he once bought. Revision, professional sex-skills expert. A trapeze artist, rubber spine, spangles glued onto her like the scales of a fish. He hates these echoes. Saints used to hear them, crazed lice-infested hermits in their caves and deserts. Pretty soon he'll be seeing beautiful demons beckoning to him, licking their lips, with red hot nipples and flickering pink tongues. Mermaids will rise from the waves, out there beyond the crumbling towers, and he'll hear their lovely singing and swim out to them and be eaten by sharks. Creatures with the heads and breasts of women and the talons of eagles will swoop down on him, and he'll open his arms to them, and that will be the end. Brainfrizz. Or worse, some girl he knows, or knew, will come walking towards him through the trees, and she'll be happy to see him but she'll be made of air. He'd welcome even that, for the company.

★**tart** prostitute
spangles (pl) *Pailetten*
lice pl of louse
★**to beckon** to give signs that sb should approach
talons (pl) claws

He scans the horizon, using his one sunglassed eye: nothing. The sea is hot metal, the sky a bleached blue, except for the hole burnt in it by the sun. Everything is so empty. Water, sand, sky, trees, fragments of past time. Nobody to hear him.

"Crake!" he yells. "Asshole! Shit-for-brains!"

What does Jimmy, the protagonist of the novel, blame Crake for?

He listens. The salt water is running down his face again. He never knows when that will happen and he can never stop it. His breath is coming in gasps, as if a giant hand is clenching around his chest – clench, release, clench. Senseless panic. "You did this!" he screams at the ocean.

No answer, which isn't surprising. Only the waves, wish-wash, wish-wash. He wipes his fist across his face, across the grime and tears and snot and the derelict's whiskers and sticky mango juice. "Snowman, Snowman," he says. "Get a life."

Bonfire

Once upon a time, Snowman wasn't Snowman. Instead he was Jimmy. He'd been a good boy then.

Jimmy's earliest complete memory was of a huge bonfire. He must have been five, maybe six. He was wearing red rubber boots with a smiling duck's face on each toe; he remembers that, because after seeing the bonfire he had to walk through a pan of disinfectant in those boots. They'd said the disinfectant was poisonous and he shouldn't splash, and then he was worried that the poison would get into the eyes of the ducks and hurt them. He'd been told the ducks were only like

What might be the function of the disinfectant?

pictures, they weren't real and had no feelings, but he didn't quite believe it.
So let's say five and a half, thinks Snowman. That's about right.

The month could have been October, or else November; the leaves still turned colour then, and they were orange and red. It was muddy underfoot – he must have been standing in a field – and it was drizzling. The bonfire was an enormous pile of cows and sheep and pigs. Their legs stuck out stiff and straight; gasoline had been poured onto them; the flames shot up and out, yellow and white and red and orange, and a smell of charred flesh filled the air. It was like the barbecue in the backyard when his father cooked things but a lot stronger, and mixed in with it was a gas-station smell, and the odour of burning hair.
Jimmy knew what burning hair smelled like because he'd cut off some of his own hair with the manicure scissors and set fire to it with his mother's cigarette lighter. The hair had frizzled up, squiggling like a clutch of tiny black worms, so he'd cut off some more and done it again. By the time he was caught, his hair was ragged all along the front. When accused he'd said it was an experiment. [...]

*charred** scorched, burned

At the bonfire Jimmy was anxious about the animals, because they were being burned and surely that would hurt them. No, his father told him. The animals were dead. They were like steaks and sausages, only they still had their skins on.
And their heads, thought Jimmy. Steaks didn't have heads. The heads made a difference: he thought he could see the animals looking at him reproachfully out of their burning eyes. In some way all of this – the bonfire, the charred smell, but most of all the lit-up, suffering animals – was his fault, because he'd done nothing to rescue them. At the same time he found the bonfire a beautiful sight – luminous, like a Christmas tree, but a Christmas tree on fire. He hoped there might be an explosion, as on television.
Jimmy's father was beside him, holding on to his hand. "Lift me up," said Jimmy. His father assumed he wanted to be comforted, which he did, and picked him up and hugged him. But also Jimmy wanted to see better.
"This is where it ends up," said Jimmy's father, not to Jimmy but to a man standing with them. "Once things get going." Jimmy's father sounded angry; so did the man when he answered.

Why was this "bonfire" made?

reproachfully expressing disapproval or blame

*luminous** glowing, radiant, bright

What is suspected by the two grown-ups?

"They say it was brought in on purpose." "I wouldn't be surprised." said Jimmy's father. "Can I have one of the cow horns?" said Jimmy. He didn't see why they should be wasted. He wanted to ask for two but that might be pushing it.
"No," said his father. "Not this time, old buddy." He patted Jimmy's leg.
"Drive up the prices," said the man. "Make a killing on their own stuff, that way."
"It's a killing all right," said Jimmy's father in a disgusted tone. "But it could've been just a nutbar. Some cult thing, you never know."
"Why not?" said Jimmy. Nobody else wanted the horns. But this time his father ignored him.
"The question is, how did they do it?" he said. "I thought our people had us sealed up tight as a drum."
"I thought they did too. We fork out enough. What were the guys doing? They're not paid to sleep."
"It could've been bribery," said Jimmy's father. "They'll check out the bank transfers, though you'd have to be pretty dumb to stick that kind of money into a bank. Anyway, heads will roll."
"Fine-tooth comb, and I wouldn't want to be them," said the man. "Who comes in from outside?" "Guys who repair things. Delivery vans." "They should bring all that in-house."
"I hear that's the plan," said his father. "This bug is something new though. We've got the bioprint." "Two can play at that game," said the man. "Any number can play," said Jimmy's father.

nutbar madman

★**bribery** corruption

fine-tooth comb here: thorough search

Paradice project
Margaret Atwood: Oryx and Crake

What is "Crake's life work"?

[...] Now, said Crake, it was time to get serious. He was going to show Jimmy the other thing they were doing – the main thing, here at Paradice. What Jimmy was about to see was ... well, it couldn't be described. It was, quite simply, Crake's life work. Jimmy put on a suitably solemn face. What next? Some gruesome new food substance, no doubt. A liver tree, a sausage vine. Or some sort of zucchini that grew wool. He braced himself.
Crake led Jimmy along and around; then they were standing in front of a large picture window. No: a one-way mirror.

★**gruesome** horrible

★**to brace oneself** here: to pluck up one's courage, to take heart

Jimmy looked in. There was a large central space filled with trees and plants, above them a blue sky. (Not really a blue sky, only the curved ceiling of the bubble-dome, with a clever projection device that simulated dawn, sunlight, evening, night. There was a fake moon that went through its phases, he discovered later. There was fake rain.)

That was his first view of the Crakers. They were naked, but not like the Noodie News: there was no self-consciousness, none at all. At first he couldn't believe them, they were so beautiful. Black, yellow, white, brown, all available skin colours. Each individual was exquisite. "Are they robots, or what?" he said.

"You know how they've got floor models, in furniture stores?" said Crake.

"Yeah?"

"These are the floor models."

It was the result of a logical chain of progression, said Crake that evening over drinks in the Paradice Lounge (fake palm trees, canned music, real Campari, real soda). Once the proteonome had been fully analyzed and interspecies gene and part-gene splicing were thoroughly underway, the Paradice Project or something like it had been only a matter of time. What Jimmy had seen was the next-to-end result of seven years of intensive trial-and-error research. "At first," said Crake, "we had to alter ordinary human embryos, which we got from – never mind where we got them. But these people are *sui generis*. They're reproducing themselves, now."

"They look more than seven years old," said Jimmy.

Crake explained about the rapid-growth factors he'd incorporated. "Also," he said, "they're programmed to drop dead at age thirty – suddenly, without getting sick. No old age, none of those anxieties. They'll just keel over. Not that they know it; none of them has died yet."

"I thought you were working on immortality."

"Immortality," said Crake, "is a concept. If you take 'mortality' as being, not death, but the foreknowledge of it and the fear of it, then 'immortality' is the absence of such fear. Babies are immortal. Edit out the fear, and you'll be ..." [...]

Other Compounds in other countries were following similar lines of reasoning, said Crake, they were developing their own prototypes, so the population in the bubble-dome was ultra-secret. Vow of silence, closed-circuit internal e-mailing only unless you had special permission, living quarters inside the security zone but outside the airlock. This would reduce the chances of infection in case any of the staff got sick; the

❶ Who are the "Crakers"?

Noodie News author-coined term: newscast with naked newsreaders

self-consciousness *Verlegenheit*

floor model example on display

canned music particularly soothing or lulling music as is often played in supermarkets

proteonome author-coined scientific neologism

splicing connecting, joining together

sui generis (Latin) forming a class of own

to incorporate here: to include

to keel over to fall over, drop dead

Compounds here: competitors of "Paradice", the company Crake and Jimmy are working for

enhanced improved

Rejoov from to rejuvenate: to make someone look and feel younger; "Rejoov" is a company cooperating with "Paradice"

top brass executive staff (coll.)
to jump the gun to do something too soon (coll.)

doing the ads Jimmy is working for "Paradice" as an advertising expert.

★**blend** mixture, combination

hit-or-miss random, inaccurate

spoilage damaged goods

docility submissiveness, obedience
insect repellant substance that drives away insects
★**unrefined** not purified
innate inborn

BlyssPluss Pill another invention of Crake's: a stimulating feel-good wonder pill, which, on the one hand, increases sexual desire and voluptuousness, on the other, makes people sterile and solves the problem of overpopulation

★**interim** temporary
★**stupendous** amazing, enormous
inextricably not able to be separated
haphazard random, irregular, lacking direction

Paradice models had enhanced immune-system functions, so the probability of contagious diseases spreading among them was low.

Nobody was allowed out of the complex. Or almost nobody. Crake could go out, of course. He was the liaison between Paradice and the Rejoov top brass, though he hadn't let them in yet, he was making them wait. They were a greedy bunch, nervous about their investment; they'd want to jump the gun, start marketing too soon. Also they'd talk too much, tip off the competition. They were all boasters, those guys.

"So, now that I'm in here I can never get out?" said Jimmy. "You didn't tell me that".

"You'll be an exception," said Crake. "Nobody's going to kidnap you for what's inside your skull. You're just doing the ads, remember?" But the rest of the team [...] was confined to base for the duration.

"The duration?"

"Until we go public," said Crake. Very soon, RejoovenEsense hoped to hit the market with the various blends on offer. They'd be able to create totally chosen babies that would incorporate any feature, physical or mental or spiritual, that the buyer might wish to select. The present methods on offer were very hit-or-miss, said Crake: certain hereditary diseases could be screened out, true, but apart from that there was a lot of spoilage, a lot of waste. The customers never knew whether they'd get exactly what they'd paid for; in addition to which, there were too many unintended consequences.

But with the Paradice method, there would be ninety-nine per cent accuracy. Whole populations could be created that would have pre-selected characteristics. Beauty, of course; that would be in high demand. And docility: several world leaders had expressed interest in that. Paradice had already developed a UV-resistant skin, a built-in insect repellant, an unprecedented ability to digest unrefined plant material. As for immunity from microbes, what had until now been done with drugs would soon be innate.

Compared to the Paradice Project, even the BlyssPluss Pill was a crude tool, although it would be a lucrative interim solution. In the long run, however, the benefits for the future human race of the two in combination would be stupendous. They were inextricably linked – the Pill and the Project. The Pill would put a stop to haphazard reproduction, the Project would replace it with a superior method. They were two stages of a single plan, you might say.

It was amazing – said Crake – what once-unimaginable things had been accomplished by the team here. What had been altered was nothing less than the ancient primate brain. Gone were its destructive features, the features responsible for the world's current illnesses. For instance, racism – or, as they referred to it in Paradice, pseudospeciation – had been eliminated in the model group, merely by switching the bonding mechanism: the Paradice people simply did not register skin colour. Hierarchy could not exist among them, because they lacked the neural complexes that would have created it. Since they were neither hunters nor agriculturalists hungry for land, there was no territoriality: the king-of-the-castle hard-wiring that had plagued humanity had, in them, been unwired. They ate nothing but leaves and grass and roots and a berry or two; thus their foods were plentiful and always available. Their sexuality was not a constant torment to them, not a cloud of turbulent hormones: they came into heat at regular intervals, as did most mammals other than man. In fact, as there would never be anything for these people to inherit, there would be no family trees, no marriages, and *no* divorces. They were perfectly adjusted to their habitat, so they would never have to create houses or tools or weapons, or, for that matter, clothing. They would have no need to invent any harmful symbolisms, such as kingdoms, icons, gods, or money. Best of all, they recycled their own excrement. By means of a brilliant splice, incorporating genetic material from …

"Excuse me," said Jimmy. "But a lot of this stuff isn't what the average parent is looking for in a baby. Didn't you get a bit carried away?"

"I told you," said Crake patiently. "These are the floor models. They represent the art of the possible. We can list the individual features for prospective buyers, then we can customize. Not everyone will want all the bells and whistles, we know that. Though you'd be surprised how many people would like a very beautiful, smart baby that eats nothing but grass. The vegans are highly interested in that little item. We've done our market research."

Oh good, thought Jimmy. Your baby can double as a lawnmower.

"Can they speak?" he asked.

"Of course they can speak," said Crake. "When they have something they want to say."

"Do they make jokes?"

❶ What advantages over "normal" people are the "Crakers" supposed to have?

to register to notice

to plague to cause constant problems

***turbulent** causing disturbance

***to come into heat** to enter the state of being prepared for sexual activity (in female animals)

***icons** images, statues, (religious) idols

splice process of joining genetic material from different sources

***to customize** to adapt, make personal adjustments to suit the customer's personal needs and wishes

all the bells and whistles all features that the models have to offer

vegans vegetarians who do not eat any animal products

★malice *Boshaftigkeit*

cork-nut Jimmy's nickname

"Not as such," said Crake. "For jokes you need a certain edge, a little malice. It took a lot of trial and error and we're still testing, but I think we've managed to do away with jokes." He raised his glass, grinned at Jimmy. "Glad you're here, cork-nut," he said. "I needed somebody I could talk to."

★dimples (pl) *Grübchen*

The dimples of DelGlacey

M. T. Anderson: Feed

M. T. Anderson is the author of the young adult novels *Thirsty* (1998) and *Burger Wuss* (1999). He studied English literature at Harvard and Cambridge universities, and received an MFA in Creative Writing from Syracuse University. He is currently on the faculty of Vermont College's MFA Program in Writing for Children and lives in Boston, MA. His novel *Feed* (2004) was a finalist for the National Book Award, a Boston Globe-Horn Book Honor Book and the winner of the Los Angeles Times Book Prize for Young Adult Fiction. In this satire, Anderson imagines a future society dominated by the Feed – a next-generation Internet/television hybrid that is directly built into people's brains when they are babies. The Feed, an information stream dominated by corporations, has an omnipresent ability to categorize human thoughts and desires. The result is a consumer society driven by fashion and shopping and the pursuit of entertainment. *Feed* tells the story of teenage narrator Titus, whose ability to read, write and think for himself has been nearly destroyed by the advertising-laden Internet feed. It also deals with his relationship with Violet, who rebels against the state of denial in which the rest of society is living and who challenges him to question their world.

How are schools of the past portrayed in contrast to School™?

TM abbreviation for trademark; in *Feed*, School™ is a product like any other

meg mega, very large

Okay, but sometimes, though, I did get worried that she was too smart for me.

I don't do too good in School™. We were back in School™, so I was reminded pretty often that I was stupid.

School™ is not so bad now, not like back when my grandparents were kids, when the schools were run by the government, which sounds completely like, Nazi, to have the government running the schools? Back then, it was big boring, and all the kids were meg null, because they didn't learn anything useful, it was all like, da da da da, this happened in fourteen ninety-two, da da da da, when you mix like, chalk and water, it makes nitroglycerin, and that kind of shit? And nothing was useful?

Now that School™ is run by the corporations, it's pretty brag, because it teaches us how the world can be used, like mainly how to use our feeds. Also, it's good because that way we know that the big corps are made up of real human beings, and not just jerks out for money, because taking care of children, they care about America's future. It's an investment in tomorrow. When no one was going to pay for the public schools anymore and they were all like filled with guns and drugs and English teachers who were really pimps and stuff, some of the big media congloms got together and gave all this money and bought the schools so that all of them could have Computers and pizza for lunch and stuff, which they gave for free, and now we do stuff in classes about how to work technology and how to find bargains and what's the best way to get a job and how to decorate our bedroom.

It was still hard, there were some times when none of us did good, and I felt stupid, and we all felt stupid, and Loga and Calista were like, Omigod! This is so dumb!

Could the teacher be any more, please, condescending?

Omigod, I know. Like, thanks for the heapin' helpings of a yawn banquet.

And I sat there with my palms pressed into my forehead, thinking about Violet, at home, being smart, I would think about some conversation we were having where I was dumb. Like she was always reading things about how everything was dying and there was less air and everything was getting toxic. She told me about how things were getting really bad with some things in South America, but she couldn't really tell exactly how bad, because the news had been asked to be a little more positive. She said that it made her frightened to read all this kind of thing, about how people hated us for what we did. So one time I said to her that she should stop reading it, because it was just depressing, so she was like, But I want to know what's going on, so I was like, Then you should do something about it. It's a free country. You should do something. She was like, Nothing's ever going to happen in a two-party system. She was like, da da da, nothing's ever going to change, both parties are in the pocket of big business, da da da, all that? So I was like, You got to believe in the people, it's a democracy, we can change things.

She was like, It's not a democracy.

I hated it when she got like this, because then she wasn't like herself, I mean she wasn't like this playful person who drags

pretty brag exceptionally good (coll.)

corps here: corporations

congloms large corporations and companies

***condescending** patronizing

➊ In what ways do the narrator Titus and his girlfriend Violet differ from each other?

➋ How are their differences reflected in their style of speech?

underground here: hidden, covert
ribbing material with raised strips

me around the mall doing crazy shit, she was suddenly like those girls in School™ who sit underground and dress all in black with ribbing and get an iron fixture for their jaws and they're like, "Capitalist fool-propaganda tool," holding up both their hands, etc. When she said things like, It's not a democracy, suddenly I couldn't stand to be having this whole conversation. I was like, Oh, yeah, and she was like, It's not, and I was like, Oh, okay, and she said, No, it's not a democracy, and I was like, Yes, it is, and she was like, No it isn't, and I got sarcastic, so I was like, No, sure, it's all fascist, isn't it? We're all fascists? Then she was like, really gently, No, please, I'm not trying to be an asshole. It's not a democracy.

I was like, Then what is it?

A republic. It's a republic.

Why?

Because we elect people to vote for us. That's my point.

So why is it like that?

Because if it was a democracy, everybody would have to decide about everything.

I thought about that. We could have everybody vote. From the feeds. Instantaneous. Then it would be a democracy.

*__instantaneous__ at once, immediate

Except, she said, only about seventy-three percent of Americans have feeds.

Oh, I said. Yeah. And so I felt stupid. There's that many who don't?

Then she told me, I didn't use to have a feed.

I was like, What do you mean?

She was quiet like she didn't want to chat. It was that kind of quiet. Then she went, We didn't have enough money. When I was little. And my dad and mom didn't want me to have one.

Holy shit.

I got it when I was seven.

I'm sorry, I said.

For what?

For not knowing. You know, that so many people don't have them.

No one with feeds thinks about it, she said. When you have the feed all your life, you're brought up not to think about things. Like them never telling you that it's a republic and not a democracy. It's something that makes me angry, what people don't know about these days. Because of the feed, we're raising a nation of idiots. Ignorant, self-centered idiots.

Suddenly, she realized what she had said, that she'd just called me a self-centered, ignorant idiot. She stopped. She started stumbling all over her words, and she was like, I didn't mean … I, you know … it's not really important, but just, I believe …, and so on. I just sat there and watched her. I could tell I was liking to watch her trip over her words while I was doing this angry face, so I didn't move my mouth or chat her or anything. I just sat, and she felt bad, and then she even chatted me, I'm sorry, which was bad, because it showed that we both knew I was stupid, and then I looked away. I looked away, and she put her hand on my arm, which was the worst, because it was the consolation prize.

That night, when I got home, I was looking out the window, being sorry, and my mother was like, "What's wrong?"

I didn't answer for a while. Finally, I said, "Do you think I'm stupid? I mean, am I dumb?"

"You're a nontraditional learner."

Smell Factor said, "No, he's not. He's dumb."

My mother asked, "Is this re: Violet?"

"No."

"Come on. Is it re: her? Because she shouldn't make you feel stupid. That's not good."

"Mom, it's un-re: her, okay?"

"She should be proud of you."

I didn't want to say anything. I didn't want my mom to think Violet was a snob. I was just dumb.

My mom came over and said to me, "You're a wonderful boy. I know I'm your mom, but I can say that you're a wonderful boy. Isn't he, Steve?"

My dad was conked out at the table going over the news on the feed, but he pulled himself up, and she was like, "Isn't he a wonderful boy?," and my mom was like, "You're as handsome as a duck in butter."

"Where does she live, anyway?" my dad asked.

"I don't know. Like, two hundred miles from here. I've never been there. Why?"

"Just asking."

"You're a catch," said my mother. "You're pewter."

That was no help at all, and the next day, I did really bad on a test, and I came home, and Violet chatted me to say she couldn't talk, she was, I didn't know, learning ancient Swahili or building a replica of Carthage out of iron filings or finding the cure for entropy or some shit, and I was sitting around, staring at a corner of the room, where two of the walls and the floor came together, and my mom and dad

consolation prize small prize given to someone who has not won the competition or the race

Smell Factor nickname of Titus' brother

re: author-coined: due to, because of, in reaction to

to be conked out slang: half-asleep due to exhaustion

pewter *Preispokal*

filings small pieces of metal

entropy disorder or randomness of a system

caught me doing it, and my mom came up and hugged me. I could tell it was all staged. They'd tried to find me. I patted Mom a little on the back, enough to say, Okay, yeah, enough for affection. You can back off now, Ma. She did, and I hoped they would leave, but they weren't done. So I had to sit there and listen to about me.

How do his parents first try to console him?

She said, "You're just the boy we wanted. You're good enough for any girl. You're just what we asked for."

My dad was meg uncomfortable and kept on moving from foot to foot.

My mom ran her fingers through my hair, and rocked me back and forth, even though I was standing, and she said, like a poem, "You've got your father's eyes and my nose."

"And my mouth," said my dad.

"And my hands," said my mom.

"And the chins, dimples, and hairline of DelGlacey Murdoch."

"What?" I said.

"This big actor," explained my mom. "We thought he was like the most beautiful man we'd ever seen in our lives."

"Well," said my dad, "we thought he was going to be big."

"We saw a feedcast with him in it the night we ... the night you were made." My mom winked.

"What?" I said. "What was his name? You never told me about the actor."

"He was ... What did you say his name was again, Steve?"

"DelGlacey Murdoch."

"DelGlacey Murdoch," said my mom, kind of smoothing things over. "That's right. And we thought he was the most beautiful man we'd ever seen. So after the movie we went right to the conceptionarium and told them, 'We want the most beautiful boy you've ever made. We want him with my nose and his dad's eyes, and for the rest, we have this picture of DelGlacey Murdoch."

conceptionarium author-coined term for the place where children are conceived, or rather, 'produced'

I said, "I've never even heard of DelGlacey Murdoch."

My father played nervously with his pinstripes. "He didn't ... he didn't really take off the way we expected. After that movie, he was mostly ... I guess ... small roles."

"He starred in some things," said my mom. "Steve, he starred in a lot of things."

"Straight to daytime," said my dad.

"Honey, he was the most beautiful actor ever. So we went into the conceptionarium, and told the geneticists what we wanted, and your father went in one room, and I went in the other, and ..."

geneticist scientist who specializes in genetics

"Hey – hey – I don't want to hear!"
"You know what he was in?" said my dad. "Remember Virtual Blast? He played the fifth Navy Seal, with the croup. You know, coughing."
"He was in the feature with all the crazy utensils," said my mother. "A few years ago? That one? He was the doorman in the pillbox hat."
I had already pulled up a list of his feed-features and I was going over them. None of them got more than two stars. My parents were checking my feed, I could feel them like prodding it, and my mom was like, "It doesn't matter what he was in," and she chatted something to my dad, and so he was like, "No, no, that isn't the point."
"What we're talking about," said my mother, "is how handsome you are, and how brave you are."
"We've decided that you've been through a lot," said my father. "You've been very brave," my mother repeated.
"Yeah ... ?" I said. "I just fell down. The guy touched me and I just like, fell down."
"You were brave," said my father.
"We've decided you need a little cheering up," said my mother. I started to feel a little better. I could feel their feeds shifting towards a common point, some kind of banner they were pulling up.
"We've decided to get you your own upcar," said my mother.
"You can pick it," said my dad. "Within certain limits."
"Oh, god!" I said. "Oh, god! Oh, Mom – Dad – this is – oh, shit! Holy shit! Are you kidding! You're like the best mom and dad ever!"
"We're not kidding," said my dad. "Here's the banner."
And it unwrapped in my head, a banner for a dealer, and links to other dealers, and a big line of credit, and I was hugging them, and I was like holy shit, by tomorrow I would be driving to pick up Violet in my own goddamn upcar, and suddenly, suddenly, I didn't feel so stupid anymore.

croup *(asthmaartige) Krupp-Krankheit*

pillbox hat *Pagenkappe*

***to prod** to push, stimulate

brave mutig

What is their second, more successful attempt like?

upcar author-coined term for flying cars

banner here: advertisement

I love my wife
Robert Sheckley: The Perfect Woman

Mr Morcheck awoke with a sour taste in his mouth and a laugh ringing in his ears. It was George Owen-Clark's laugh, the last thing he remembered from the Triad-Morgan party. And what a party it had been! All Earth had been celebrating the turn of the century. The year Three Thousand! Peace and prosperity to all, and happy life ...

"How happy is your life?" Owen-Clark had asked, grinning slyly, more than a little drunk. "I mean, how is life with your sweet wife?"

That had been unpleasant. Everyone knew that Owen-Clark was a Primitivist, but what right had he to rub people's noses in it? Just because he had married a Primitive Woman ...

"I love my wife," Morcheck had said stoutly. "And she's a hell of a lot nicer and more responsive than that bundle of neuroses you call *your* wife."

But of course, you can't get under the thick hide of a Primitivist. Primitivists love the faults in their women as much as their virtues – more, perhaps. Owen-Clark had grinned ever more slyly, and said. "You know, Morcheck, old man, I think your wife needs a checkup. Have you noticed her reflexes lately?" Insufferable idiot ! Mr Morcheck eased himself out of bed, blinking at the bright morning sun which hid behind his curtains. Myra's reflexes – the hell of it was, there was a germ of truth in what Owen-Clark had said. Of late, Myra had seemed rather – out of sorts.

"Myra!" Morcheck called. "Is my coffee ready?" There was a pause. Then her voice floated brightly upstairs. "In a minute!" Morcheck slid into a pair of slacks, still blinking sleepily.

Thank Stat the next three days were celebration-points. He'd need all of them just to get over last night's party.

Downstairs Myra was bustling around, pouring coffee, folding napkins, pulling out his chair for him. He sat down, and she kissed him on his bald spot. He liked being kissed on his bald spot.

"How's my little wife this morning?" he asked.

"Wonderful, darling," she said after a little pause. "I made Seffiners for you this morning. You like Seffiners."

Morcheck bit into one, done to a turn, and sipped his coffee. "How do you feel this morning?" he asked her.

Myra buttered a piece of toast for him, then said, "Wonderful, darling. You know, it was a perfectly wonderful party last night. I loved every moment of it."

"I got a little bit veery", Morcheck said with a wry grin.

"I love you when you're veery." Myra said. "You talk like an angel – like a very clever angel, I mean. I could listen to you forever." She buttered another piece of toast for him.

Mr Morcheck beamed on her like a benignant sun, then frowned. He put down his Seffiner and scratched his cheek.

stoutly resolutely, with courage

*__neuroses__ (pl) collection of mental disorders involving physical and emotional symptoms such as bodily pain, depression etc.

*__insufferable__ unbearable, unendurable

germ microbe, microorganism; here: a litte bit

out of sorts not oneself, often due to illness

slacks casual trousers

to bustle to move busily

*__bald__ hairless

done to a turn cooked just right

veery a North American bird, noted for its songs performed at dusk; here obviously meaning tipsy or drunk

wry twisted, ironic

benignant kind, favourable

"You know," he said, "I had a little ruck-in with Owen-Clark. He was talking about Primitive Women."

Myra buttered a fifth piece of toast for him without answering, adding it to the growing pile. She started to reach for a sixth, but he touched her hand slightly. She bent forward and kissed him on the nose.

"Primitive Women!" she scoffed. "Those neurotic creatures! Aren't you happier with me, dear? I may be Modern – but no Primitive Woman could love you the way I do – and I adore you!"

What she said was true. Man had never, in all recorded history, been able to live happily with unreconstructed Primitive Woman. The egoistic, spoiled creatures demanded a lifetime of care and attention. It was notorious that Owen-Clark's wife made him dry the dishes. And the fool put up with it! Primitive Women were forever asking for money with which to buy clothes and trinkets, demanding breakfast in bed, dashing off to bridge games, talking for hours on the telephone, and Stat knows what else. They tried to take over men's jobs. Ultimately, they proved their equality.

Some idiots like Owen-Clark insisted on their excellence.

Under his wife's enveloping love, Mr Morcheck felt his hangover seep slowly away. Myra wasn't eating. He knew that she had eaten earlier, so that she could give her full attention to feeding him. It was little things like that that made all the difference.

"He said your reaction time had slowed down."

"He did?" Myra asked, after a pause. "Those Primitivists think they know everything."

It was the right answer, but it had taken too long. Mr Morcheck asked his wife a few more questions, observing her reaction time by the second hand on the kitchen clock. She *was* slowing up. "Did the mail come?" he asked her quickly. "Did anyone call? Will I be late for work?"

After three seconds she opened her mouth, then closed it again. Something was terribly wrong.

"I love you," she said simply.

Mr Morcheck felt his heart pound against his ribs. He loved her! Madly, passionately! But that disgusting Owen-Clark had been right. She needed a checkup. Myra seemed to sense his thought. She rallied perceptibly, and said, "All I want is your happiness, dear. I think I'm sick ... Will you have me cured? Will you take me back after I'm cured – and not let them change me – I wouldn't want to be changed!" Her bright head sank on her arms. She cried noiselessly, so as not to disturb him.

ruck-in fight

★**to scoff** to mock, ridicule

notorious well-known

to put up with sth to accept

trinkets (pl) trifles, things of little value

to dash off to leave quickly

to seep to leak gradually

➔ What seems to be wrong with Myra?

★**hand** here: pointer on a clock

to rally here: to recover

★ **coarse** crude, rough, strong
mental fiber basic character, essential structure
prone disposed (here: to ailments like Myra's)
★ **stamina** persistence, ability to endure unfavourable conditions

"It'll just be a checkup, darling," Morcheck said, trying to hold back his own tears. But he knew – as well as she knew – that she was really sick.

It was so unfair, he thought. Primitive Woman, with her coarse mental fiber, was almost immune to such ailments. But delicate Modern Woman, with her finely balanced sensibilities, was all too prone. So monstrously unfair! Because Modern Woman contained all the finest, dearest qualities of femininity. Except stamina.

Myra rallied again. She raised herself to her feet with an effort. She was very beautiful. Her sickness had put a high color in her cheeks, and the morning sun highlighted her hair.

"My darling," she said. "Won't you let me stay a little longer? I may recover by myself." But her eyes were fast becoming unfocused.

"Darling ..." She caught herself quickly, holding on to an edge of the table. "When you have a new wife – try to remember how much I loved you." She sat down, her face blank.

"I'll get the car," Morcheck murmured, and hurried away. Any longer and he would have broken down himself.

Walking to the garage he felt numb, tired, broken. Myra – gone! And modern science, for all it great achievements, unable to help.

He reached the garage and said, "All right, back out." Smoothly his car backed out and stopped beside him.

"Anything wrong, boss?" His car asked. "You look worried. Still got a hangover?"

"No – it's Myra. She's sick."

The car was silent for a moment. Then it said softly, "I'm very sorry, Mr Morcheck. I wish there were something I could do."

"Thank you," Morcheck said, glad to have a friend at this hour.

"I'm afraid there's nothing anyone can do."

The car backed to the door and Morcheck helped Myra inside. Gently the car started.

It maintained a delicate silence on the way back to the factory.

V. Utopia or dystopia in poetry and song

Guess it's time for the Judgement Day

Zager and Evans: In the Year 2525

Zager and Evans were a Lincoln, Nebraska rock-pop duo of the late 1960s and early 1970s named after its two members, Denny Zager and Rick Evans.
They are best known for *In the Year 2525*, written by Rick Evans, a song warning against the dangers of technology. *In the Year 2525* hit number one on the charts in 1969. (It was number one on the day that Neil Armstrong and Buzz Aldrin first set foot on the moon.)

In the year 2525
If man is still alive.
If woman can survive, they may find.
In the year 3535
Ain't gonna need to tell the truth, tell no lies.
Everything you think, do and say, is in the pill you took today.
In the year 4545
Ain't gonna need your teeth, won't need your eyes.
You won't find a thing to chew.
Nobody's gonna look at you.
In the year 5555
Your arms hanging limp at your sides.
Your legs got nothing to do.
Some machine doing that for you.
In the year 6565
Ain't gonna need no husband, won't need no wife.
You'll pick your son, pick your daughter too.
From the bottom of a long glass tube. Whoa-oh
In the year 7510
If God's a-comin, he oughta make it by then.
Maybe he'll look around himself and say.
Guess it's time for the Judgment Day.
In the year 8510
God is gonna shake his mighty head.

Name three technological inventions and their consequences as envisioned in this song.

***limp** lame, stiff

He'll either say. I'm pleased where man has been.
Or tear it down and start again. Whoa-oh
In the year 9595
I'm kinda wonderin' if man is gonna be alive.
He's taken everything this old Earth can give.
And he ain't put back nothing. Whoa-oh

Explain "He's taken everything this old Earth can give. And he ain't put back nothing."

Now it's been ten thousand years
Man has cried a billion tears.
For what he never knew,
now man's reign is through.
But through eternal night.
The twinkling of starlight.
So very far away.
Maybe it's only yesterday.

In the year 2525
If man is still alive.
If woman can survive, they may find.

In the year 3535 [fade]

Hey Mr. Dinosaur
The Police: Walking in Your Footsteps

The Police

The Police, a progressive pop band made up of Stewart Copeland, former English Literature teacher Sting (born Gordon Sumner) and Andy Summers, became famous for their nervous and punky, reggae-injected pop/rock music. As their career progressed, The Police grew considerably more adventurous, experimenting with jazz and various world music influences. Their Album *Synchronicity* was released in 1983 and became a multi-platinum success in both Europe and the U.S.. By the time the band separated in 1985, The Police were one of the world's most popular bands.

Fifty million years ago
You walked upon the planet so,
Lord of all that you could see
Just a little bit like me,
Walking in your footsteps.

Hey Mr. Dinosaur
You really couldn't ask for more.
You were God's favorite creature
But you didn't have a future,
Walking in your footsteps.

Hey mighty brontosaurus,
Don't you have a lesson for us
You thought your rule would always last

➔ Why are humans and dinosaurs compared in this song?

Why is the line 14 also a warning for the future of the human race? ➔

Who are "they"? ➔

There were no lessons in your past
You were built three stories high
They say you would not hurt a fly
If we explode the atom bomb,
Would they say that we were dumb?

Walking in your footsteps.

Fifty million years ago
They walked upon the planet so
They live in a museum
It's the only place you'll see 'em.

Walking in your footsteps ...

*meek poor, humble, gentle

Explain the relevance of "The meek shall inherit the earth" with regard to this song. ➔

They say the meek shall inherit the earth ...

Walking in your footsteps ...

They ... earth (l. 25) from the Gospel of Matthew 5:5 in the New Testament, also known as one of the most famous of the Beatitudes. In the King James Version of the Bible the text reads: Blessed are the meek: for they shall inherit the earth.

It starts with an earthquake

REM: It's the End of the World (As We Know It)

REM

Formed in Athens, Georgia, USA in 1980, REM became, with the release of their first single *Radio Free Europe* (1981), an immediate favourite in the alternative, independent rock music scene, which is largely distributed through small, independent record labels, college radio stations and small concert venues. Although the group has since become one of the most successful mainstream bands, it is acknowledged to have been one of the forerunners of the thriving alternative rock movement during the '90s.

That's great, it starts with an earthquake, birds and
snakes, an aeroplane and Lenny Bruce is not afraid.
Eye of a hurricane, listen to yourself churn – world
serves its own needs, don't misserve your own needs.
Feed it off an aux speak, grunt, no, strength, Ladder
start to clatter with fear fight down height.
Wire in a fire, representing seven games, a government
for hire and a combat site. Left of west and coming in
a hurry with the furies breathing down your neck.
Team by team reporters baffled, trumped, tethered crop.
Look at that low plane! Fine, then. Uh oh,
overflow, population, common food, but it'll do.
Save yourself, serve yourself. World serves its own needs,
listen to your heart bleed. Tell me with the rapture and
the reverent and the right, right. You vitriolic,

Lenny Bruce US comedian 1925–1966, whose daring, experimental and often obscene form of entertainment caused him to be in constant trouble with the law

to churn to shake violently
to misserve to serve unfaithfully
aux abbreviation for auxiliary, i.e. helpful support
★**baffled** confused, shocked
trumped outdone, defeated
tethered tied with a rope
rapture ecstasy, extreme joy
reverent deeply respectful
vitriolic sarcastic

slam slang: severe criticism
psyched intimidated, frightened

patriotic, slam, fight, bright light, feeling pretty psyched.

It's the end of the world as we know it.
It's the end of the world as we know it.
It's the end of the world as we know it and I feel fine.

slash gash, wound, cut
★**to escalate** to make worse, increase
to incinerate to burn to ashes
votive small church candle representing a wish or desire
★**renegade** traitor, deserter
★**to decline** to go down, decrease

Six o'clock – TV hour. Don't get caught in foreign towers. Slash and burn, return, listen to yourself churn. Locking in, uniforming, book burning, blood letting. Every motive escalate. Automotive incinerate. Light a candle, light a votive. Step down, step down. Watch your heel crush, crushed, uh-oh, this means no fear cavalier. Renegade steer clear! A tournament, tournament, a tournament of lies. Offer me solutions, offer me alternatives and I decline.

It's the end of the world as we know it.
It's the end of the world as we know it.
It's the end of the world as we know it and I feel fine.

continental drift divide The Earth's surface is constantly moving and dividing.
Leonid Brezhnev General Secretary of the Communist Party of the Soviet Union from 1964 to 1982.
Lester Bangs Influential American music journalist, author and musician, 1948–1982, who died of an overdose of drugs.

The other night I dreamt of knives, continental drift divide. Mountains sit in a line, Leonard Bernstein. Leonid Brezhnev, Lenny Bruce and Lester Bangs. Birthday party, cheesecake, jelly bean, boom! You symbiotic, patriotic, slam book neck, right? Right.

It's the end of the world as we know it.
It's the end of the world as we know it.
It's the end of the world as we know it and I feel fine ... fine ...

(It's time I had some time alone)

This is my nirvana
Alanis Morissette: Utopia

Alanis Morissette

Alanis Morissette was born in 1974 in Ottawa, Canada. She showed a love for singing and songwriting at an early age. When she was 9 years old, Morissette wrote her first song. In 1992, she was nominated for three Juno Awards: Single of the Year, Best Dance Record, and Most Promising Female Vocalist (which she won). Her album *Jagged Little Pill*, 1995, sold over 30 million copies worldwide and won Grammy awards for Album of the Year, Best Female Rock Vocal Performance, Best Rock Song and Best Rock Album. The song *Utopia* was first released on the album *Under Rug Swept* in 2002.

We'd gather around all in a room fasten our belts engage in dialogue
We'd all slow down rest without guilt not lie without fear disagree sans judgement

sans French: without

We would stay and respond and expand and include and allow and forgive and enjoy and evolve and discern and inquire and accept and admit and divulge and open and reach out and speak up

*__to evolve__ to develop, gradually change, mature
to discern to perceive, recognize
to divulge to reveal, disclose

This is utopia this is my utopia
This is my ideal my end in sight
Utopia this is my utopia
This is my nirvana
My ultimate

nirvana in Hinduism: heavenly state that exists beyond the cycle of reincarnation, paradise

We'd open our arms we'd all jump in we'd all coast down into safety nets

to coast here: to move easily

We would share and listen and support and welcome be propelled by passion not invest in outcomes we would breathe and be charmed and amused by difference be gentle and make room for every emotion

to be propelled to be moved forward

We'd provide forums we'd all speak out we'd all be heard we'd all feel seen

We'd rise post-obstacle more defined more grateful we would heal be humbled and be unstoppable we'd hold close and let go and know when to do which we'd release and disarm and stand up and feel safe

*__humbled__ here: aware of one's blessings

This is utopia this is my utopia
...

I don't want my daddy leaving home tonight

Faithless: Mass Destruction

Faithless

Faithless are a UK group of musicians whose music is described as a cross between trip-hop and dance. The Song *Mass Destruction* was first released on their album *No Roots* in 2004.

Which weapons of mass destruction does the songwriter name?

soaraway band-invented term: flown away

Whether long range weapon or suicide bomber
A wicked mind is a weapon of mass destruction
Whether your soaraway Sun or BBC 1
Misinformation is a weapon of mass destruction
You're called a Caucasian or a poor Asian
Racism is a weapon of mass destruction
Whether inflation or globalization
Fear is a weapon of mass destruction

My dad came into my room holding his hat
I knew he was leaving,
He sat on my bed told me some facts, son.
I have a duty, calling on me
You and your sister be brave my little soldier
And don't forget all I told ya
You're the mister of the house now remember this
And when you wake up in the morning give ya momma a kiss
Then I had to say goodbye

In the morning I woke momma with a kiss on each eyelid,
Even though I'm only a kid
Certain things can't be hid
Momma grabbed me
Held me like I was made of gold
But left her in the story untold
I said, momma it will be alright
When daddy comes home, tonight

Whether Halliburton or Enron or anyone
Greed is a weapon of mass destruction

We need to find courage, overcome
Inaction is a weapon of mass destruction

My story stops here, let's be clear
This scenario is happening everywhere
And you ain't going to nirvana or favana
You're coming right back here to live out your karma
With even more drama than previously, seriously
Just how many centuries have we been
Waiting for someone else to make us free
And we refuse to sleep
The people overseas are just like we
Mad leadership, amigos, unfettered and free
They feed on the people they're supposed to lead
I don't need it
I don't mean for people to pray away
For the lord to make it straight
It's only now we do it right
Cos I don't want my daddy, leaving home tonight.

➔ Where does the father have to go?

ya slang for: your

Halliburton is one of the world's largest providers of products and services to the oil and gas industries. The company has been criticized for its close ties to the US government.
Enron The bankruptcy of Enron, one of the world's leading electricity, natural gas, and communications companies, led to thousands of employees losing their life savings in 2001.

favana name of a Byzantine crypt in Veglie, Italy, used by hermits in the 8th century; here obviously standing for (a way to enter) paradise

karma in Buddhism and Hinduism sum of a person's actions believed to decide his fate in the next life

unfettered unhindered, not restrained
cos slang for: because

Thou art past the tyrant's stroke

William Shakespeare: Fear No More the Heat o' the Sun

Fear no more the heat o' the sun,
Nor the furious winter's rages;
Thou thy worldly task hast done,
Home art gone, and ta'en thy wages;
Golden lads and girls all must,
As chimneys-sweepers, come to dust.

Fear no more the frown o' the great;
Thou art past the tyrant's stroke:
Care no more to clothe and eat;
To thee the reed is as the oak:
The scepter, learning, physic, must
All follow this, and come to dust.

Fear no more the lightning-flash,
Nor the all-dreaded thunder-stone;
Fear not slander, censure rash;
Thou hast finished joy and moan;
All lovers young, all lovers must
Consign to thee, and come to dust.

No exorciser harm thee!
Nor no witchcraft charm thee!
Ghost unlaid forbear thee!
Nothing ill come near thee!
Quiet consummation have;
And renownéd be thy grave!

ta'en taken
reed *Schilf*
oak *Eiche*
scepter symbol of royalty
slander defamation, false statement
censure rash harsh criticism
to charm to bewitch
unlaid not pacified, still haunting the earth seeking peace of mind
to forbear to suppress
consummation perfection, completion

Definitions

Utopia

The noun *"utopia"* refers to human efforts to create a perfect society that does not exist (yet).
Ideas which could radically change our world for the better but are very difficult or impossible to realize are often labelled as *"utopian"*.

Origin of the word "Utopia"

The term "utopia" was first coined by Sir Thomas More as part of the title of his book *De Optimo Reipublicae Statu deque Nova Insula Utopia* (circa 1516), commonly known as *Utopia*.
The term is combined from two Greek words: ου τοπος, ου "not" and τοπος "place". Utopia therefore means "nowhere" or "non-existent place". But there is more to it: More created the neologism (new word or expression, invented by the author) "utopia" from two existing Greek words: outopia (no place) and its homophone eutopia (good place).
In the 19th century, the concept of a utopian society became closely connected with *socialist ideas* such as an egalitarian distribution of goods (i.e. everybody gets the same), often with a total abolition of money, and citizens only doing work which they enjoyed and which was for the common good, leaving them with plenty of time to enjoy the arts and study the sciences.
Especially after the two world wars, a *global utopia of world peace* was optimistically seen as one of the possible endings of history.
In addition to this, there have always been *religious utopias,* most often described as a garden of delights, a life free of worry in the middle of streets paved with gold.
A *scientific and technological utopia* is the strong belief that one day science and technology will allow utopian living standards, like the absence of death, illness and suffering, and changes in human nature and the human condition.

Dystopia

A dystopia, also called *anti-utopia* or *cacotopia* (alternative spelling: *kakotopia*), is the antithesis of the utopian society. It is usually characterized by a totalitarian or authoritarian form of government or some other kind of oppressive control.
Writers of dystopian literature mostly engage their readers with something that is familiar to them since the dystopian society must have echoes of the readers' own experiences. Only if the

readers can identify the patterns that might lead to the dystopia they are confronted with, can their reading become an involving and effective experience.

Some typical traits of dystopian literature:

- War, revolution, rebellion, overpopulation, natural disaster or other climactic events have resulted in dramatic changes to society.
- The standard of living among the bulk of the population is generally poorer than in contemporary society. Only the ruling class is living in luxury. (An exception to this is, for example, *Brave New World*, where all people enjoy a higher standard of living in exchange for a loss in intelligence, emotion and freedom).
- The reader is confronted with a protagonist who questions this society because he/she feels that something is terribly wrong.
- Since most dystopian literature is set in the future, it often features technology more advanced than that of contemporary society. Usually, this advanced technology is controlled exclusively by the ruling class and used to help them to stay in power.

Acknowledgements

Texts

Book of Isaiah: King James Version of the Bible, Jove edition, New York, Declair Publishing Company 1977, pp. 483, 488, 501

The Qur'an: The Holy Qur'an, translated by Abdullah Yusuf Ali, Wordsworth Classics of World Literature, Hertfordshire, Ware 2000, pp. 6, 435, 465f.

Plato: The Republic, translated by G. M. A. Grube (Hackett 1992); reprinted by permission of Hackett Publishing Company, Inc. All rights reserved; selections from pp. 95–97 (Book III), pp. 132–134 (Book V)

Thomas More: Utopia, translated by Gilbert Burnet in 1684, Stillwell/KS USA, Digireads.com Publishing 2005, pp. 65–66

Tommaso Campanella: The City of the Sun, translated with introduction by Daniel J. Donno, London, The University of California Press, Ltd. 1981, pp. 37, 53–55, 59, 61–63

Jonathan Swift: Gulliver's Travels, New York, Airmont Publishing Co. 1963, pp. 55–60

Herbert George Wells: The Time Machine, © 1984 Philipp Reclam jun. GmbH & Co., Stuttgart, pp. 45–50, 89–92, 97–98; © für den Text: The Executors of the Estate of the Late H. G. Wells. Abdruck mit Genehmigung von A. P. Watt Ltd., London

Aldous Huxley: Brave New World, A Triad Panther Book, London/ Toronto/Sydney/New York, Granada Publishing 1977, pp. 15–25

George Orwell: 1984, Signet Classic (no. 451 – CY 688) from New American Library Of World Literature, Inc., New York, pp. 5–8

Margaret Atwood: The Handmaid's Tale, London, Vintage 1996, pp. 180–192

Larry and Andy Wachowski: The Matrix, http://www.script-o-rama.com/snazzy/dircut.html; © Warner Brothers

Margaret Atwood: Oryx and Crake, London, Virago Press 2004, pp. 11–21 (text pp. 63–66); pp. 355–360 (text pp. 66–70)

M. T. Anderson: Feed; Text © 2003 M. T. Anderson; extract from *Feed* by M. T. Anderson; reproduced by permission of Walker Books Ltd, London SE11 5HJ

Robert Sheckley: The Perfect Woman, from: Isaac Asimov/Groff Conklin (editors): 50 Short Science Fiction Tales, 1963, pp. 238–241

(Denny) Zager and (Rick) Evans: In the Year 2525, RCA Records 1969; text: Richard Evans; © by Chelsea Music Publ.; für D: Edition Nordton Rolf Budde Musikverlag GmbH, Berlin

The Police: Walking in Your Footsteps, Words and Music by Sting, Synchronicity, A & M Records, Inc., 1983; © Gordon M. Sumner; für D: EMI Music Publishing Germany GmbH & Co. KG, Hamburg

REM: It's the End of the World (As We Know It), Michael Stipe, Album Document, I.R.S. Records, 1987; text: William Thomas Berry/Peter Lawrence Buck/Michael E. Mills/John Michael Stipe; © Night Garden Music; für D: NEUE WELT MUSIKVERLAG GMBH, Hamburg

Alanis Morissette: Utopia, from the Album Under Rug Swept, 2002; text: Alanis Nadine Morissette; © 1974 Music; für D: Universal Music Publ. GmbH/MCA Music GmbH; Berlin

Faithless: Mass Destruction, from the Album No Roots, 2004; text: Rollo Armstrong/Ayalah Deborah Bentovim/Maxi Jazz; © BMG Music Publ. Ltd./Champion Music/Warner Chappell Music; für D: Musik-Edition Discoton GmbH (BMG Music Publ. Germany) München; NEUE WELT MUSIKVERLAG GMBH, Hamburg; Sony/ATV Music Publishing (Germany) GmbH, Berlin

William Shakespeare: Fear No More the Heat o' the Sun, from: Cymbeline, Act IV, Scene 2, 324–347, ca. 1609; The Complete Works of William Shakespeare, edited by Sybil Thorndike, Murrays Sales and Service Co., London 1974, p. 1006

Illustrations

p. 6: © akg-images/Nimatallah; p. 16: © AKG, Berlin; p. 18 and 20: © akg-images; p. 23: © dpa, Frankfurt; p. 28: © AKG, Berlin; p. 37: © ullstein bild; p. 41 and 52: © dpa-Fotoreport; p. 81, 83 and 86: © dpa-Fotoreport; p. 85: © dpa